D0075009

PROPERTY OF
BAKER COLLEGE-FLINT

The American Heritage Series

OSKAR PIEST, *General Editor*

[NUMBER ELEVEN]

EDWARD BELLAMY
On Religion and Society

EDWARD BELLAMY
On Religion and Society

EDWARD BELLAMY

SELECTED WRITINGS ON
RELIGION AND SOCIETY

Edited with an Introduction by

JOSEPH SCHIFFMAN
Associate Professor of English
Long Island University

GREENWOOD PRESS, PUBLISHERS
WESTPORT, CONNECTICUT

Library of Congress Cataloging in Publication Data

Bellamy, Edward, 1850-1898.
    Selected writings on religion and society.

    Half title: On religion and society.
    Reprint of the ed. published by Liberal Arts Press,
New York, which was issued as no. 11 of the American
heritage series.
    Bibliography: p.
    1. Religion and sociology--Collected works.
I. Title. II. Title: On religion and society.
[B945.B41S35 1974]   081   74-40
ISBN 0-8371-7359-0

Copyright 1955 The Liberal Arts Press, Inc.

Originally published in 1955 by The Liberal Arts Press,
New York.

Reprinted with the permission of The Liberal Arts Press, Inc.

Reprinted from an original copy in the collections of the
University of Illinois Library.

Reprinted in 1974 by Greenwood Press,
A division of Congressional Information Service, Inc.
88 Post Road West, Westport, Connecticut 06881

Library of Congress catalog card number 74-40
ISBN 0-8371-7359-0

Printed in the United States of America

10 9 8 7 6 5 4 3 2

ACKNOWLEDGMENTS

The editor wishes to express grateful acknowledgment to the following for permission to use Bellamy materials in this anthology: to the Houghton Library, Harvard University, for selections from the Bellamy Collection, the William Dean Howells Collection, and the T. W. Higginson Papers; to Arthur E. Morgan for *The Religion of Solidarity by Edward Bellamy;* to Marion Bellamy Earnshaw, the daughter of Edward Bellamy, and to Bellamy Earnshaw, his grandson, for their manuscript copy of Edward Bellamy's Book Reviews and Editorials; and to the editors of *PMLA* (*Publications of the Modern Language Association of America*), and *American Quarterly* (the official journal of the American Studies Association), for sections from articles by this editor which first appeared in those magazines.

J. S.

CONTENTS

EDWARD BELLAMY'S SELECTED WRITINGS ON RELIGION AND SOCIETY

INTRODUCTION

I

"How soon could you bring it out?" Edward Bellamy anxiously queried Ticknor, the publisher. "Now is the accepted time, it appears to me, for publications touching on social and industrial questions to obtain a hearing." [1] Bellamy hung on the answer, for *Looking Backward,* the book under discussion, germinated from his tight-lipped agony over "the unspeakable abomination of the actual universe." Personal and public developments encouraged Bellamy to hope that his private mood might strike a public chord. It did—*Looking Backward* became "perhaps the most influential book of the late nineteenth century, which expressed most deeply its hopes and aspirations. . . ." [2]

The birth of his two children had thrown the frail Bellamy into troubled concern for their future, and 1886, "the year of ten thousand strikes," [3] taught him that his own problem of security was a general one. So, taking pen in hand in the fall of the year, he tried "to reason out a method of economic organization by which the republic might guarantee the livelihood and material welfare of its citizens." He compounded his thought in the form of a "sugar-coated pill," as his widow explained to me (in conversations, 1950-1952), to entice large numbers of readers. Under the sugar-coating, however, were imperishable, precious materials—an all-consuming religious desire for the social good, hitherto only partially and privately expressed, and an amazingly advanced kind of learn-

[1] See Caroline Ticknor, *Glimpses of Authors* (Boston, 1922), pp. 112-121.

[2] Lewis Mumford, "Mirror of a Violent Half Century," *New York Times,* Jan. 15, 1950, Sec. 7, p. 1.

[3] The telling phrase of Allan Seager, *They Worked for a Better World* (New York, 1939), p. 108.

ing, dearly bought at the price of health and normal social life. *Looking Backward* stemmed from the deepest recesses of the author's heart and mind, producing a classic in man's concern for man.

II

In boyhood manuscripts, several signed "Bellamie" (French for "fine friend"), young Edward, son of the Baptist minister at Chicopee Falls, Massachusetts, had earnestly taken upon his young shoulders weighty problems in history, religion, family life, government, and qualities of people. The parsonage provided the proper note of high dedication as young Edward worked at the journals and notebooks he was to keep all his life, the confidants of his "careless, reckless, drunken, blasphemous moods."

Searching for dedicated spirits in history, twelve-year-old Bellamy seized upon Mahomet, and, in a long essay surprisingly free of any narrow churchly consideration, he extolled historical Islamism:

Could Mahomets motive have been a bad one in establishing this religion. Forty years old when he received his first revelation and for years after did he with a few followers wander from city to city pursued thence by his numberous enemies. Despised of all men. What worldly motive could have led him to persevere. . . . What but the greatest faith in the divine authenticity of his mission . . . could have enabled him to bear up under the storm of persecution which he and his doctrines encountered. When to have supported the prevailing religion would have gained him Wealth Influence and a high position. . . . His not doing so ought to be conclusive proofs that Mahomet at least believed the doctrines he taught. . . . This Religion certainly was well adapted to take a hold upon the feelings of the Asiatics. . . . But considering there to be three great religions Christian Islam, and Pagan, Islamism holds and certainly ought to hold the second rank. . . .[1]

[1] The Bellamy Collection, Houghton Library, Harvard University, bMS Am 1181.4 MSS 24. Throughout this introduction, Bellamy's MSS are reproduced as they appear in the original, with only slight editing.

In his broad appreciation of the historical process, the young minister's son had included paganism as one of the "three great religions." The reader cannot help speculating on what the Reverend Rufus Bellamy, the boy's father, would have thought of that, or, if he approved, what his congregation would have said!

One wonders what force or circumstance stirred the mind of young Edward. The outward events of his life afford little clue. So bare are they in suggestion that Arthur E. Morgan, author of *Edward Bellamy* (1944), often lamented the difficulty of writing a biography.

Born March 26, 1850 into an old New England family, young Bellamy could trace his ancestral line through clergymen and merchants back to his great-great-grandfather, the Reverend Joseph Bellamy, noted colonial divine and associate of Jonathan Edwards. While many of young Bellamy's ancestors had followed the ministry, they generally exhibited an independent, deviant quality. The Reverend Benjamin Putnam, young Bellamy's grandfather on his mother's side, was forced to resign his pastorate at Salem, Massachusetts, after joining the Masons, and the Reverend Rufus Bellamy, the author's father, was denied his pulpit at Chicopee Falls for unascertainable reasons after thirty-four years of service. The Bellamy family, deeply religious, knew the pleasures and trials of church life; and young Edward was to learn them, too.

He was reared along orthodox, Calvinist lines with emphasis on prayer, self-examination, and earnest respectability. While Edward's father was "jolly," and doubtful of hell-fire and eternal damnation, his mother's spirit, more strongly Calvinist, prevailed. Mrs. Maria Bellamy supervised the upbringing of her children, and when she talked with her son, Edward, "it was nearly always about religious and spiritual matters" (Morgan, p. 25), since initiation into the Baptist sect of believers could come only after many anxious hours of soul-searching. Bellamy's friend and biographer, Mason Green, wrote of the consummate experience: "Edward had serious moments about his . . . conversion. . . . His mother prayed for it, his father preached for it . . . and he stood up in a protracted meeting at the age of fifteen, confessed and repented . . . and was comforted. . . ." [2]

But comfort in the traditional faith of his family did not remain long with Bellamy. He lived in an age of violent change, when the religious life of the Connecticut Valley underwent severe questioning. In a little-known fantasy, "With The Eyes Shut," he pictured the bewildering religious controversy of the New England of his day in the form of talking clocks: "There were religious and sectarian clocks, moral clocks, philosophical clocks, free-thinking and infidel clocks, literary and poetical clocks, educational clocks, frivolous and bacchanalian clocks. . . . In startling proximity to the religious department I was shown the skeptical clocks. So near were they, indeed, that when, as I stood there, the various time-pieces announced the hour of ten, the war of opinions that followed was calculated to unsettle the firmest convictions. The observations of an Ingersoll which stood near me were particularly startling. . . ." [3] Here Bellamy spoke humorously about his most troublesome (and fruitful) mood —religious doubt.

In the privacy of his notebooks and journals we find him moving from a moment of questioning traditional theology toward a determined rejection, and, then, a final break with the church. That Bellamy's religious pilgrimage was painful is made clear in these revealing lines from his notebook: "Tell me for God['s] sake something of God. I have been hound[ed?] out of the church. I know nothing of the doctrine" (Notebook B, p. 5). And further along, this strange, touching fragment:

[2] "Edward Bellamy: a Biography." Ch. 1, The Bellamy Collection. (Subsequent references to The Bellamy Collection appear in the text of this introduction.)

[3] Reprinted in *The Blindman's World and Other Stories by Edward Bellamy* (Boston, 1898), pp. 347-348.

Our Father in Heaven, Hallowed be Thy name, Thy
Kingdom come,
Thy will be done on earth as it is . . .
Edward Bellamy
Wavering Wavering Bellamy Blubber Edward Bellamy [.]
(Binder 3-B, Miscellaneous Fragments)

What do these cryptic scribblings mean? It is impossible to
know the full story since Bellamy was loath to publicize
"supreme matters." He never discussed his notebooks and
journals or showed them to anyone. His religious battles were
fought in private, and many of them never saw paper.

However, here is a fragment which supplies a basis for the
development of Bellamy's opposition to the church: "Ordinary
religion is different in degree (not as it should be in kind)
from loyalty to earthly sovereigns" (Notebook 4, p. 21). He,
who had bowed his head in conversion, now apparently re-
sented such obeisance. Finally, the shattering fragment: "I
don't know how a man can better serve his country than by
becoming an Infidel" (Notebook 4, p. 11).

Why had traditional faith become inadequate for Bellamy?
The answer must be sought in whispers from his notebooks
and journals; in his published writings, especially *Looking
Backward* and *Equality;* and in the public records of his life
and time. These all suggest a man tortured by the spectacle of
"man's inhumanity to man." On a student trip to Europe in
1868, he had become aware of poverty for the first time, and
upon his return home he recognized the seeds of European
development in American life: "Although it had required
the sights of Europe to startle me to a vivid realization of
the inferno of poverty beneath our civilization, my eyes having once been opened, I had now no difficulty in recognizing
in America, and even in my own comparatively prosperous
village, the same conditions in course of progressive development." [4]

Chicopee Falls, Bellamy's home village, had become in-

[4] Reprinted in *Edward Bellamy Speaks Again!* (Kansas City, 1937), pp.
217-229.

dustrialized before his birth. Its water power attracted Boston industrialists who, between 1820 and 1850, had converted the peaceful farming area into an industrial community. A student of the area writes: ". . . there was no smooth economic progression from stage to stage. . . . The few farmers and the foundrymen of the neighborhood looked upon a kind of industrial activity of which they had never seen the like. A long narrow cotton mill paralleled the newly-built canal. Rows of tenements arose alongside the mill . . . looking as though a section of a distant city had been lifted and transplanted bodily to Chicopee Falls. . . . The village was now the home of a corporation." [5] Industrial sores festered in Chicopee— long hours of work, crowded tenements, epidemics, unemployment, strikes, shifting populations. Furthermore, the seventies were a time of depression and steadily lowering standards of living. Throughout the Connecticut Valley, poverty was plainly visible.

As a working newspaperman, Bellamy himself saw the human cost of the Industrial Revolution. In an editorial for the *Springfield Daily Union* he wrote feelingly of child labor in the mills: "What . . . shall we say of the children of this misery? . . . Any day at noon you can see them in dingy flocks, hovering along the sidewalks between their boarding place and 'the yard.' . . . The mere sight of them; so old and worn and miserable to look at, yet so young, is proof enough that a great wrong exists somewhere among us which is inflicting a vast amount of barbarity, a positive cruelty of monstrous proportions upon these children and others like them in New England. . . ." [6]

Probably Bellamy had been thinking of these stunted factory children when he mounted the lecture platform of the Chicopee Village Lyceum in 1872 to deliver a public address, apparently his first, entitled "The Barbarism of Society."

[5] Vera Shlakman, "Economic History of a Factory Town: A Study of Chicopee, Massachusetts," *Smith Coll. Studies in Hist.*, XX, 1-4 (Oct. 1934-July 1935), 25, 48.

[6] "Overworked Children in Our Mills," June 5, 1873, p. 2.

Lamenting the "slavery" of poor laborers, he asked passionately, "Have the ardent longings of the lovers of men been
toward an unattainable felicity? Are the aspirations after
liberty, equality, and happiness implanted in the very core of
our hearts for nothing?" [7] How could a minister's son who
fervently believed in the Brotherhood of Man and the
Fatherhood of God find solace in a society which had not yet
learned all the lessons of love?

III

Among Bellamy's manuscripts deposited at Harvard is an
unfinished semi-autobiographical novel, variously entitled
"Eliot," "Caesar," or "Eliot Carson." Obviously, Bellamy
worked long and hard over this novel, leaving at least nine
unfinished versions, but he never completed it to his satisfaction. The story has Edna Damon, a noble young lady, as a
main character. Plagued by religious doubts, she visits her
minister, Dr. Fenno, and confides to him that she cannot pray
any longer, although prayer used to be "ecstasy" for her. She
is plagued by "awful facts—the blind brutality, the hideous
cruelty of life, the utter immorality of the conditions of
existence, facts that make it atrocious blasphemy to talk of a
responsible deity . . . [when] the only piety possible for us is
to deny the existence of an Almighty God out of very respect
for his character." Dr. Fenno attempts to console Edna by
speaking of his faith, but Edna feels that his faith is blind,
that it asks the faithful to believe that "tears are not tears,
that blood is not blood, that death is not death." The minister
reminds Edna of the doctrine of compensation, but she refuses
to accept this as her philosophy, and announces she is determined to leave the church: "And now as to my leaving the
church, I feel it my duty to do so, because I am living a lie
in pretending to hold to a creed that I have ceased to believe.
Do not believe that I shall ever give over the search for God.
I shall never do that. I do not know anything else save that

[7] Reprinted in *Edward Bellamy Speaks Again!* pp. 218-221.

search that is worth while on earth" (Notebook 3, pp. 69-75, 77).

By leaving the church, Edna brings social ostracism upon herself. Implored to maintain church membership without belief, she feels her integrity violated, and leaves for the countryside to rest, think, and search for faith. Like Edna, Bellamy had been reared to find "ecstasy" in prayer, but had now ceased to believe in the church; and, like Edna, he continued to search for a faith.

In the countryside Edna meets young Eliot Carson, a hermit who has renounced a promising career in a mill to devote his life to leisurely meditation, nature, and the development of his soul. Edna, distressed and floundering, finds Eliot certain and at peace. They speak of their religious histories, and Eliot confides to Edna that he has found a new faith to live by, one that may help her too: "This is the new religion I have to offer you—a religion which instead of adding to the vain attempts to explain . . . God tells you that you are more God than man . . ." (Notebook 3, p. 111). Here Bellamy expressed the central core of his developing faith.

Bellamy used the idea of man's divinity as the theme of a remarkably fine essay, "The Religion of Solidarity." [1] In this essay, written in 1847 when he was only twenty-four years old but never published in his lifetime, Bellamy expressed what he later described as "the germ of . . . my philosophy of life." Here he renounced the Calvinist God of the hostile universe, puny man, and individual fate, to reaffirm the secular American religion of man as an element of the divine. Bellamy's "Religion of Solidarity" is strongly reminiscent of Emerson, Whitman, and, particularly, Henry James, Senior, and opens a path leading from transcendentalism to the utopianism of *Looking Backward*.

In Emersonian tones, Bellamy sketches a friendly universe beckoning to man, but one that saddens man because he cannot enter into perfect physical and mental communion with it. Man's spirit is also rankled by time. He would merge

[1] See pp. 3-27.

with the past and future as well: ". . . [standing] before some
. . . monument of old life . . . some dead city or deserted site.
. . . We are conscious of a sense of loss . . . at having had no
part in the skein of life that once . . . tangled on this very
spot. We are conscious of a repining at the barrier of time
that has included and shut us up in today. The experience is
very similar when, as we muse earnestly on the glories of
future ages, the vision of the world to be rises before us, and
we feel that in essence we belong no more to today than to
yesterday and tomorrow. . . . Hungry, not for more life, but
for all the life there is, we count ourselves robbed of the days
when we were not and those in which we shall not be. . . ." [2]

Bellamy, like Emerson, believed man's spiritual tendency
toward universal experience was to find satisfaction in future
development of his potential. In "The Religion of Solidarity"
Bellamy demonstrates why the historical climb of man will
carry him into even higher spheres of the spirit:

> . . . this tendency of the human soul to a more perfect realiza-
> tion of its solidarity with the universe . . . is already . . . a
> matter of history. I would call attention to the fact that senti-
> mental love of the beautiful and sublime in nature, the charm
> which mountains, sea, and landscape so potently exercise upon
> the modern mind through a subtle sense of sympathy, is a
> comparatively modern and recent growth of the human mind.
> The ancients knew, or at least say, nothing of it. It is a curious
> fact that in no classical author are to be found any allusions
> to a class of emotions and sentiments that take up such large
> space in modern literature. It is almost within a century, in
> fact, that this susceptibility of the soul seems to have been
> developed. . . . If culture can add such a province as this to
> human nature within a century, it is surely not visionary to
> count on a still more complete future development of the
> same group of subtle psychical faculties.[3]

Solidarity with the universe would bring a life of beauty.
Like Walt Whitman, Bellamy pointed to sexual union as the
faintest, yet most suggestive, glimpse into the ravishing nature
of the merging of souls:

[2] See pp. 4-5.
[3] See pp. 11-12.

The sexual relation is the greatest example of that physical correlation which, approximating the individualities and relaxing the rigor of their natural attitude of mutual antagonism and exclusiveness, affords an opportunity for the confluence in at least a partial sympathy of the roles of lovers, and the bliss resulting from the consciousness of even this imperfect union is a proof of the common essence of souls. But after all, how imperfect is this union, even when helped to the utmost by physical conditions. . . . There is a lust of soul for soul dwarfing the lust of body for body, as the universal dwarfs the individual; a lust insatiable, a passion hopeless yet entrancing, sweeter in desire than all others in consummation. . . .[4]

And, exactly like Henry James, Senior, Bellamy celebrated love of the human race as the essence of the religious spirit: ". . . that cardinal motive of human life . . . is a tendency and a striving to absorb or be absorbed in or united with other lives and all life. . . . It is the operation of this law in great and low things, in the love of men for women, and for each other, for the race, for nature, and for those great ideas which are the symbols of solidarity, that has ever made up the web and woof of human passion. . . . As individuals we are indeed limited to a narrow spot in today, but as universalists we inherit all time and space." [5]

The son of the Baptist minister at Chicopee Falls had developed a faith on which to base his life. Locating the source of spirit and life outside the individual, it denied the possibility of individual redemption or a churchly elect. Affirming the evolutionary potentials of spiritual man, it denied the restrictive morbidity of original sin. Dedicated to a full life in this world, it denied the all-consuming appeal of an afterworld. Moved by love of man, it was the simplest of faiths, yet the most complex to live by; the oldest of faiths, it required continual reaffirmation in the face of scorn.

While Bellamy's religious pilgrimage from an old to a new

4 See p. 19.
5 See p. 18 and pp. 24-25.

faith was silent, desperate, and lonely, it was actually part of a broad movement reshaping religious thinking. Post-Civil War America earnestly questioned traditional concepts of Christianity. Bellamy himself, as a newspaper editor, welcomed such discussion as a hopeful augury: ". . . the changes toward more philosophical and liberal ways of holding Christian doctrines going on within the church simultaneously with the unexampled attacks from without, are a better indication that a perfected Christianity will survive the shock than would be a greater stiffness in maintaining the ancient doctrines in unmitigated rigor. . . ." [6] Bellamy here pinned his faith on the development of the New Theology. The movement toward a more liberal theology excited him. In several places in his notebooks and journals he speaks with great admiration of the Reverend Henry Ward Beecher, pioneer in liberal Christian theology (e.g., Notebook 3, p. 86).

The movement Beecher represented was broad, involving many ministers from Bellamy's native Massachusetts. In Springfield, Washington Gladden lamented the old faith's "individualistic approach," and Theodore T. Munger of North Adams sought to build a concept of the solidarity of the human race to replace excessive individualism. New England factory life prompted such a development in thought. The same forces that had led the churchgoing Bellamy to break with the church led others inside the church to reshape their thinking.

The academic center for the New Theology was Andover Seminary in industrial Massachusetts.[7] Founded in 1808 by Massachusetts Calvinists to defend the old faith, Andover, by 1884, had become "a militant apostle" of the New Theology. The factories of nearby Lawrence, which Andover students could easily see, changed theological concepts in much the same way that the factories of Chicopee had changed Bellamy's

---

[6] *Springfield Daily Union*, March 13, 1875, p. 6.

[7] See Daniel Day Williams, *The Andover Liberals: A Study in American Theology* (New York, 1941).

thought. The New Theology was the life-or-death response of liberal Protestant sects toward deep-going nineteenth-century changes and intellectual pressures.

The secular figure of Bellamy's day who did most to alter ideas of the spiritual was Auguste Comte, whose writings Bellamy read. Comte provided the central spiritual theme for the Victorian age in his "Religion of Humanity." He emphasized, as Bellamy was later to do, the solidaristic concept of living for others as well as living in the past and in the future, and came to the conclusion that humanity fulfilled the place of God. The nineteenth century, under the impact of the Industrial Revolution, steadily moved away from a heaven-centered faith to an earth-centered faith, and the theory of evolution supplied the necessary justification for altering this most traditional of concepts.

IV

But Bellamy withheld his most provocative thoughts from publication. "The Barbarism of Society" was a speech delivered before a neighborly group in the Chicopee Village Lyceum; "Eliot Carson" remained a jumbled heap of variant readings; and "The Religion of Solidarity" was never offered for publication by its author. Instead of concerning himself with such challenging themes, young Bellamy, "under the sordid and selfish necessity of solving the economic problem in its personal bearings," tried law and newspaper work. After clerking in a law office in nearby Springfield for two years, he qualified for the Hampden County bar in 1871, took one case, and then gave up the law in distaste. To Bellamy, it appeared that lawyers must be callous and calculating to be successful.

Turning to newspaper work, Bellamy served on William Cullen Bryant's *New York Evening Post,* but he disliked big-city life, and returned to Springfield in June, 1872 to work as editorial writer and book reviewer for the *Springfield Daily Union.* Bellamy's newspaper work matured him by drawing him into intimate contact with the harsh industrial life of the

Springfield-Chicopee-Holyoke mill area of the Gilded Age. Also, as a book reviewer, he hungrily read and thoughtfully reviewed a flood of books by such authors as Hugo, Taine, Turgenev, Henry James, George Eliot, and Bulwer-Lytton. But, after four years of grueling newspaper work, Bellamy's health suffered, and he quit his job to travel to Hawaii in search of rest and relaxation.

When he returned home in 1878 he finished his first novel, *Six to One: A Nantucket Idyl,* a graceful tale of romantic love written with charm and ability but almost completely lacking in the kind of thought that was to bring him world-wide fame within ten years. Before writing *Six to One,* Bellamy had tried his hand at light short stories, finding the leading popular magazines of his time willing publishers. Among others, *Scribner's Monthly* had taken "The Cold Snap," "The Old Folks' Party," and "Hooking Watermelons." *Lippincott's Magazine* had accepted "A Summer Evening's Dream" and "Deserted." All these stories, like the novel, *Six to One,* were primarily designed for a romantic audience, and slighted discussion of serious problems. In several of these stories Bellamy alluded to a religion of solidarity, or tentatively sketched its outlines, but he neglected to pursue the theme in a consistently earnest manner.

The popular success of *Six to One,* however, opened up possibilities for the expression of unusual themes. Praised by critics of the *New York Nation,* the *Boston Post,* the *London Spectator,* the *Boston Transcript,* and the *Springfield Daily Union,* for his "bright," "delightful," "agreeable" tale, Bellamy turned his auspicious reception into an opportunity to treat two subjects which interested him deeply: the psychological burden of guilt, and the economic-social approach to history. Undertaking the writing of two serialized novels simultaneously, he began publishing *Dr. Heidenhoff's Process* in the *Springfield Union* on December 18, 1878, and *The Duke of Stockbridge* in the *Berkshire Courier* on January 1, 1879. Although he found the pressure of meeting two deadlines burdensome, complaining to friends of feeling harassed, he produced two volumes that students of American civilization should find praiseworthy. In *Dr. Heidenhoff's Process,* Bellamy pioneered in the modern psychiatric approach to emotional problems, and in *The Duke of Stockbridge* he interpreted the Shays Rebellion along lines validated by twentieth-century research.

V

Dr. Heidenhoff's Process [1] tells the story of Madeline Brand, a promising young person whose life is destroyed by a sense of unworthiness. The story is laid in a Massachusetts town, typical of nineteenth-century New England, where moral codes are rigidly enforced. Madeline has felt their sting. A victim of seduction, she finds life intolerable. Lacerated by the constant accusation in her mother's eyes, she escapes to Boston where she is followed by Henry Burr, a devoted beau whom she had spurned for her lover. Henry offers her love and marriage, but, unable to accept him because of her feelings of guilt and unworthiness, she sinks into deep depression.

Bellamy understood very well how feelings of guilt and self-reproach bring depression. He once wrote: "[re] . . . the Nemesis of defied prejudices . . . in age the moral conventions of childhood will reassert themselves . . . as avenging furies" (Journal 2, pp. 27-28). And even where society forgave the sinner, he might not be able to forgive himself. As Bellamy observed, "Has he lied, cheated, stolen, done meannesses? For those who do such things there is no repentance" (Journal 4, p. 3).

Society had taught the price of sin too well to Madeline. Painfully, Henry watches her sink into unrelieved depression until she almost loses consciousness of his presence. Exhausted and distraught, Henry falls asleep and dreams of a magical

[1] See pp. 80-84.

process that restores Madeline to health—Dr. Heidenhoff's process.

In a magazine article, "The Extirpation of Thought Processes. A New Invention," Dr. Heidenhoff advertises his "galvanic battery" for the annihilation of "morbid ideas." A firm believer in the "physical basis of the intellect," Dr. Heidenhoff offers to see patients at his office for treatment. After listening to Henry's account of Madeline's case, the doctor exclaims:

[In time] the mental physician will be able to extract a specific recollection from the memory. . . . Macbeth's question, "Canst thou not minister to a mind diseased; pluck from the memory a rooted sorrow; raze out the written troubles of the brain?" was a puzzler to the sixteenth-century doctor, but he of the twentieth, yes, perhaps of the nineteenth, will be able to answer it affirmatively.

Dr. Heidenhoff describes his treatment, explaining that success depends on how severely morbidity has affected the material structure of the brain. The treatment itself is simple and in no way painful. The patient's head is secured by padded clamps connected to a galvanic battery. A switch is thrown, giving the patient only a sensation of warmth, a bubbling sound in the ears, and an unpleasant taste in the mouth. The patient then falls into a deep sleep, and if he responds favorably to the treatment, awakes with a temporary feeling of slight confusion and a permanent loss of the unwanted memory. Thus, in hopeful fantasy, Bellamy foreshadowed the development of the theory and practice of modern electric convulsive ("shock") therapy.

Bellamy recognized that guilt feelings deprived people of self-respect. Dr. Heidenhoff expresses this thought succinctly: "It is the memory of our past sins which demoralizes us, by imparting a sense of weakness and causing loss of self-respect. . . . Remembered sin is the most utterly diabolical influence in the universe." In emphasizing the need for self-respect, Bellamy developed a principle basic to the theory of much

psychiatry today, so well exemplified in the writings of Harry
Stack Sullivan.[2]

Madeline hopefully undergoes Dr. Heidenhoff's process, and
awakes from the sleep induced by electric shock with the
incubus of guilt gone. Henry is elated to discover that "the
rooted sorrow" has been plucked from her mind. As her
buoyant spirits return, she and Henry prepare to marry, but
then Henry's sleep is disrupted by a messenger bearing news
of Madeline's suicide. Dr. Heidenhoff and his process was all
a dream.

The story of Madeline Brand moved William Dean Howells
deeply. Recalling his experience in reading *Dr. Heidenhoff's
Process,* Howells said:

I thought it one of the finest feats in the region of romance
. . . all the greater because the author's imagination wrought
it on the level of average life. . . . The simple people and their
circumstance were treated as if they were persons whose
pathetic story he had witnessed himself, and he was merely
telling it. He wove into the texture of their sufferings and
their sorrows the magic thread of invention so aptly and
skillfully that the reader felt nothing improbable in it. One
even felt a sort of moral necessity for it.[3]

But despite its prophetic and humane qualities, *Dr.
Heidenhoff's Process* remains a neglected novel.

The Duke of Stockbridge opens as the Minutemen of
Stockbridge march off to war on August 17, 1777. They are in
high spirits. "There was not a plowboy among the Minutemen who was not honored that day with a cordial word or
two, or at least a smile, from the magnates who never before
had recognized his existence." Bellamy unearthed a class
system in colonial Stockbridge, a "social antipodes" carried
over from Europe. Squire Woodbridge, Squire Williams,
Elisha Brown, and Squire Edwards (son of Jonathan Edwards), all men of considerable property, are the "select-

---

[2] See his *The Interpersonal Theory of Psychiatry,* edited by Helen
Swick Perry and Mary Ladd Gawel (New York, 1953).

[3] From the Prefatory Sketch to *The Blindman's World,* pp. v-vi.

men," the political, economic, and moral rulers of the village.
"The back room [of Squire Timothy Edwards' store] was, in
a sense, the council chamber, where the affairs of the village
were debated and settled by the local magnates, whose decision
the common people never dreamed of anticipating or questioning." But soon after the Revolution the social structure is
put under severe stress. Because of growing impoverization,
the "hewers of wood and the drawers of water, [the]
mechanics, farm-laborers, and farmers" begin to grumble and
question. In *The Duke of Stockbridge* the Shays Rebellion is
not a matter of simple lawlessness, but the product of economic and social forces. Bellamy discarded abstract slogans,
vividly sketching the bitterness of poverty. A sore-pressed
farmer says, ". . . we thought we wuz big pertaters, a-goin' ter
fight fer lib'ty. Wal, we licked the red-coats, and we got lib'ty,
I s'pose; lib'ty ter starve—that is, ef we don't happen ter git
sent ter jail fust." The reader is taken inside a debtor's jail to
witness the heartbreaking sufferings of the imprisoned, many
of them honored veterans of the Revolution.

The ministry and the judiciary seem deaf to the cries of the
poor, if not indeed hostile to them. By family and class lines
the ministry and judiciary are allied to the creditors. All the
institutions of power and prestige are opposed to the debtors,
or at least indifferent to their claims. None of the trusted
historians of the Shays Rebellion until Bellamy's day (e.g.,
Minot, Hildreth, Fiske, McMaster) had ever described the
grievances of the Shaysites so adequately.

The creditors of Stockbridge hunger for news from Philadelphia where the Constitutional Convention is sitting. Squire
Sedgwick expresses his hope that in Philadelphia they "will
pave the way for a stronger government . . . one that will
guarantee us not only against foreign invasion, but domestic
violence and insurrection too." Here the thesis of Charles
Beard's *An Economic Interpretation of the Constitution*
(1913) was clearly foreshadowed by Bellamy.

The debtors, with no hope of legal succor, tremble on the
brink of rebellion. In Bellamy's book the Shaysites are not in

favor of "anarchy and treason"; they are forced into rebellion to keep their farms and themselves free. Looking for a leader, the rebels of Stockbridge choose Perez Hamlin, an ex-captain in the Revolutionary Army, who had returned home to find his brother dying in a debtor's jail, and his family dangerously near losing their farm to creditors. Rallied by Perez, the debtors march off to stop the courts from sitting. They whistle a popular tune of the Stamp Act period:

> With the beasts of the wood, we will ramble for food,
> And lodge in wild deserts and caves,
> And live as poor Job on the skirts of the globe,
> Before we'll submit to be slaves, brave boys,
> Before we'll submit to be slaves.

The editor of the *Berkshire Courier* underlined Bellamy's moral purpose:

[*The Duke of Stockbridge*] has an important ethical value that must not be overlooked. Mr. Bellamy has seen more clearly than many historians and not a few political economists where to place the blame for the cruel misery that he depicts. He does not forget the principle that to whom much is given from them much is required. While never permitting us to sympathize with the crude notions, dissolute ways and bloody designs of the armed mob, he does not let us lose sight of the facts that these are but the outgrowths of an ignorance and despairing poverty that the more favored families, and even the christian [sic] church, had taken absolutely no pains to alleviate. No helping hand was extended to keep the ruined head of a household from the tax collector's or creditor's clutches; the laws, themselves a disgrace to humanity, were left to fulfil their blind and merciless course. Such men as Timothy Edwards and Parson West did not devise the prison pens, but neither did they unearth and expose their horrors to the public gaze. The theology of Calvin, Edwards and Hopkins was ably discussed but the religion of Jesus was never preached. All this could end only in tragedy when the rebellion was quelled. And the tragedy of utter despair has seldom been better portrayed, in more simple, unpretentious language . . . Perez Hamlin, the Duke of Stockbridge, disappointed in love, having seen his aged parents separated and put out to work among the town's poor, and beheld the miscarriage of all his plans, takes a last look of the pale, dead face of his brother Reub, to rescue whom from prison he had assumed the responsibility of leading the rebel mob, and then, a few hours later, is shot down among his retreating comrades in an encounter with the militia. The story is a sad one, but its lesson is one that we all, and especially those of us who are interested in the solution of social problems, may study with profit.[4]

But the novel failed to find public favor, and was not published in book form until 1900, after Bellamy's death. It seems that Bellamy himself did not appreciate the startling qualities in his single historical novel, never referring to it again after its appearance in the obscure *Berkshire Courier*. Today, however, its full merit can be gauged. While Bellamy's sympathetic view of the Shays' Rebellion placed him in a tiny minority in his own day, twentieth-century research has completely vindicated his position, raising it to the dominant one today.[5]

VI

In 1880, Bellamy experienced financial need and re-entered the newspaper world, this time as co-owner and coeditor of the *Penny News* (soon renamed the *Springfield Daily News*), with his brother Charles. Edward's role as editor quickened the maturation of his social philosophy, laying the groundwork for *Looking Backward*. In a workaday editorial, he used the figure of the old stage coach to describe the cultural lag of his day:

It is sometimes said that the world is making giant strides, that civilization is progressing at an astonishing rate, and as we read of new inventions which revolutionize branches of industry or double the speed of machinery . . . it seems as if a few years more would make the world quite a place to live in.

[4] July 2, 1879. On file at The Berkshire Athenaeum, Pittsfield, Massachusetts.

[5] For example, see James Truslow Adams, *New England in the Republic* (Boston, 1926).

But looking around us we see as much suffering and poverty, as much wretchedness and ruined life, as much starvation of soul and body, as if civilization were unknown and we were making cloth by hand and traveling by the old stage coach. . . .[1]

Six years later, he was to begin *Looking Backward* with the unforgettable analogy (one of the finest in all literature), comparing nineteenth-century society to a prodigous coach in which travelers fought for advantageous seats to avoid falling among those who strained to pull the coach up the tortuous hill.

Although his newspaper experience proved valuable, Bellamy returned to free-lance writing, turning over his share in the paper to his brother. In 1884, with the help of William Dean Howells, he published *Miss Ludington's Sister,* a novel elaborating an idea that had long intrigued him, the ever changing nature of personality, the "constant flux" in people, producing "the successive persons who constitute an individuality." While his thesis was filled with exciting potentials, he allowed it to dominate his characters so that they became distastefully perverted, sick in their obsession with self. The book, however, was a sign that Bellamy meant to keep novelizing his serious studies, just as he had done in *Dr. Heidenhoff's Process* and *The Duke of Stockbridge.*

In 1882, Bellamy had married Emma Sanderson, whom he had known since 1874. Eleven years his junior, she had lived in his father's household as a ward of the family, and, as if it were a symbol of the "home-bound pattern" of his life (Morgan, p. 148), Edward Bellamy married her and settled in his father's house.

Speaking with me in 1950, Mrs. Edward Bellamy, the author's widow, painted a picture of her husband as a lonely man who confined himself to his immediate family and books:

We lived quietly with few close friends. My husband actually discouraged visitors. Sometimes he would cry out, "Emma,

[1] *Springfield Daily News,* Dec. 10, 188(?).

please put out that light in the hall. Quick, or else someone may see it and call on us!" He seemed to want all his time for reading, thinking, or just sitting quietly at home with the family. He loved to hear me sing old church hymns to the melodeon in the parlor. But mostly he wanted to be alone, reading, or just sitting lost in thought. He kept most of his ideas to himself. Even I was surprised at discovering what *Looking Backward* contained.

While Mrs. Bellamy talked about her husband, one could not help recalling how closely he resembled his own Edna Damon who "had never particularly shone in city society. To do so involved for her too much affectation of interest in things that bored her, too much pretension of interest in people . . . too much looking wise when she did not understand, too much smiling at remarks that made her feel sad, too much simulation of agreement when she vehemently disagreed, too much silence when she wanted to cry out" (Morgan, p. 91).

By the late eighties, Bellamy's mind seemed completely taken up with social problems. Mrs. Edward Bellamy told me of her husband's personal concern over the specter of poverty and travail in the eighties:

He often seemed disturbed, concerned with a heavy problem. And he simply couldn't eat. That had been characteristic of him in all the time I knew him. . . . He would sit at the dinner table, and after carving generous slices of meat for the whole family, call out, "Mary, please bring me a glass of milk and a raw egg!" Or he would take a tumbler of whiskey. Underneath my husband's chronic refusal to eat lay a deep disturbance of spirit, I believe. I am sure he was haunted by thoughts of other people's problems, especially the poor. And that's something that fills me with wonder. Why did he feel such things so deeply when he himself had been comfortably raised and had never wanted?

Bellamy's sense of personal involvement in the poverty of other people's lives was not unique with him. The Social Gospel, essentially a middle-class Protestant movement, was beginning to involve many other people who personally "had never wanted." In reading James Dombrowski's *The Early*

Days of Christian Socialism in America (1936), one is continually struck by that fact. And Daniel Aaron's *Men of
Good Hope* (1952) stresses the middle-class origin of renowned
American radicals, reformers, and utopians. Like Bellamy,
there were many devout people, both inside and outside
churches, who keenly felt the need of a new ethic to live by,
one based upon the social teachings of Jesus. We read this
observation in Bellamy's notebook: "God holds his head low
and is the saddest being in the universe. The greatest being
. . . must be the saddest so long as there is any sadness in it.
Schopenhauer said, Pity God and so end it. We do pity God
and so improve it. This Christ tried to teach but they did not
understand" (Plots No. 2, pp. 45-46).

The decade that produced *Looking Backward,* the eighties,
saw the Social Gospel become widespread and articulate. In
the development of corporate power, great cities, and tides of
immigration, the church was called upon to play a new role.
Social Gospel literature, much like *Looking Backward* in
concern, approach, and tone, appeared in that period. In
1880, J. H. W. Stuckenberg in *Christian Sociology* asked,
"Why not make the ethics of the New Testament the test of
all social theories?" and J. H. Rylance in *Lectures on Social
Questions* called for a more co-operative society. In 1883,
Bishop Samuel Smith Harris spoke of the need for charity in
The Relation of Christianity to Civil Society. In 1885, Josiah
Strong wrote of the low state of public morals in *Our Country,*
while G. C. Lorimer's *Studies in Social Life,* Philip S. Moxom's
The Industrial Revolution, and F. N. Zabriskie's *The Bible A
Workingman's Book,* all undertook a serious analysis of
modern society from a religious standpoint. By 1886, many
social gospelers had found a reading public: T. Edwin Brown's
Studies in Modern Socialism called for an ethical, co-operative
society; A. J. F. Behrend's *Socialism and Christianity* suggested that corporations should be subject to law and the
public will; Minot J. Savage in *Social Problems* insisted that
religion should concern itself with this world; and Washington Gladden in *Applied Christianity* stated, "The Christian

moralist is . . . [obliged] to admonish the Christian employer that the wage-system, when it rests on competition as its sole basis, is anti-social and anti-Christian." In that same year, Gladden appeared as a speaker at the American Congress of Churches in Cleveland, where Henry George, another social gospeler, also spoke. And amidst rumblings from Haymarket Square, Edward Bellamy began working on *Looking Backward;* in the full tide of the Social Gospel the book appeared.

VII

Looking Backward [1] opens on a night in 1887, a year of fraud, embezzlement, theft, business failures, land-grabs, speculation, corruption, destitution, strikes, and suicides. Julian West, a wealthy, troubled Bostonian, summons a mesmerist to help him overcome insomnia. Falling into deep slumber at last, he awakes 113 years later to find himself in a wondrous Boston, a "new fraternal civilization." Under Dr. Leete's sympathetic guidance, Julian is instructed in the qualities of man's utopian age, the fruit of "the solidarity of the race and the brotherhood of man." Competition is no longer the law of the land. Instead, a new principle of social cohesion has been introduced, national co-operation, and this has stimulated all human forces into higher channels of expression and achievement. With an aching sense of pity for the nineteenth century, Julian learns of the "vast moral gap" between the social barbarism of that day, and the peaceful splendor of twentieth-century life; between reality and possibility, as Bellamy envisions it. Through Julian's eyes the reader sees how the new principle of mutual help produces marvels in all areas of life—technical, intellectual, and spiritual.

In place of the laissez faire policies of the Gilded Age, the new paternalistic state maintains an economy of abundance in which all citizens, even those infirm and insane, share equally. Pledged to the commonweal, society offers everyone suitable employment in the industrial army, retires workers

[1] See pp. 44-57, 59-76, 85-123.

at the age of forty-five, assures women independence, cooks meals in public kitchens, cleans clothes in public laundries, arranges painless shopping in giant department stores, educates everyone to ever rising standards of personal refinement and culture, and pipes exalting talk and music into private parlors. And all these epochal changes have been introduced gradually and peaceably, without rancor or violence, solely by the force of a change in public opinion. Class warfare, abhorred as a base weapon unworthy of man, has been consigned to the unhappy past.

Though impervious to the sufferings of others while living in the nineteenth century, Julian West has now developed a new sense of values. Returned, through a dream, for a horrible moment to a familiar nineteenth-century Boston slum, he suddenly recognizes the slum-dwellers as his long-denied brothers, and suffers intense personal guilt: "Therefore now I found upon my garments the blood of this great multitude of strangled souls of my brothers. The voice of their blood cried out against me from the ground. Every stone of the reeking pavements, every brick of the pestilential rookeries, found a tongue and called after me as I fled: What hast thou done with thy brother Abel?" [2] Bellamy's outraged religious consciousness echoes the cry of the eighties, "What hast thou done with thy brother Abel?" It is intriguing to watch West, fully formed by the "age of individualism," change under the impact of the "age of concert." Raised on the nineteenth-century principle of self-regard, West finds himself thinking of the needs of others, and suddenly discovers in himself a desire to contribute to the industrial pool, although he has never toiled before. The example of those around him has become infectious; West becomes an altruistic man, prefiguring theories of human personality worked out in our own day by Alfred Adler, Karen Horney, and Erich Fromm. [3]

The impact of a changed environment, one based on the

2 See p. 70.

3 See the writer's article, "Edward Bellamy's Altruistic Man," *American Quarterly,* VI (Fall, 1954), 195-209.

honor principle, can be most clearly observed in the children of Bellamy's "vision of another century." In *Equality*, the sequel to *Looking Backward*, West is surprised to discover that the children of the new society are vastly different from those he knew in the past, and concludes:

These young people had never seen coarseness, rudeness, or brusqueness on the part of anyone. Their confidence had never been abused, their sympathy wounded, or their suspicion excited. Having never imagined such a thing as a person socially superior or inferior to themselves, they had never learned but one sort of manners. Having never had any occasion to create a false or deceitful impression or to accomplish anything by indirection, it was natural that they should not know what affectation was.

Bellamy's utopia is a fascinating transformation of the millennium foretold by Hebrew prophets in the book of Daniel, and celebrated in the Psalms and in Isaiah. "The Apocalyptic Image of History," deeply embedded in the Bible, was denied in the theology of St. Augustine and Thomas Aquinas, but was revived in the Protestant Reformation by English writers of the seventeenth century.[4] Bellamy, strongly conscious of his origins, and devoted to reading the Bible as a social document, became an apocalyptic progressive, convinced that steady upward progress for the whole human race had been foretold in the Bible, and that modern events would inevitably support such prophecy. In the century that celebrated the Idea of Progress, William Dean Howells noted that Bellamy "revived throughout Christendom the faith in a millennium." While leaving the Protestant church, Bellamy carried with him its historic revival of apocalyptic faith. He himself once said: "There is no better . . . literature than the splendid poems in which Isaiah and the other Hebrew seers foretold an era when war and strife should cease, when every man should sit under his own vine and fig-tree, with none to molest or make him afraid, when the lion should lie down

[4] See Ernest Lee Tuveson, *Millennium and Utopia* (Berkeley and Los Angeles, 1949).

with the lamb, and righteousness cover the earth as the waters cover the sea. . . . Did you suppose that because . . . [this] is called the millennium, it was never coming?" [5]

Bellamy was aware that the Baptist faith of his family had played a strong role in the liberation of the peasants under feudalism, and had helped keep alive millennial hopes. His emphasis on Scripture, love for all, individual rather than church-centered faith, ethical ideals, and worldly regeneration are all reminiscent of the early Baptist faith,[6] as is his espousal in *Equality* of the "attitude of Christ toward society as an evil and perverse order of things needing to be made over." Among reading suggestions for his son, Bellamy included: "Anabaptists. Make study of these early Socialists" (Morgan, p. 146).

While Bellamy's utopia is bathed in all sorts of material delights and comforts, its central appeal is ethical. Many ministers, perceiving this, hailed Bellamy's book as "the essence of Christianity" (Dombrowski, p. 89), but the religious press, in general, attacked it. As Henry May found: ". . . most of the religious press received Bellamy's idealistic proposals either with ridicule or hostility. . . . To most churchmen, private property was sacred and government action still suspect. Yet, though only a few Christian radicals followed Bellamy, thousands of good Protestants read and discussed him." [7]

VIII

So bracing was the intellectual climate of the period that millions of Bellamy's contemporaries of all faiths read and ardently discussed *Looking Backward,* making Bellamy a household word. He was deluged with fan mail, invitations to lecture, requests for permission to translate his

[5] *Talks on Nationalism* (Chicago, 1938), pp. 66-67.

[6] See Ernst Troeltsch, *The Social Teachings of the Christian Churches,* trans. Olive Wyon (London, 1931), II, 696-697.

[7] *Protestant Churches and Industrial America* (New York, 1949), p. 158.

famous novel into foreign languages. Solicitations for articles came from Adolph J. Ochs of the *New York Times,* William Randolph Hearst of the *New York Journal,* Walter Hines Page of the *Atlantic Monthly* and the *Forum,* Edward S. Bok of the *Ladies' Home Journal,* Arthur Brisbane of the *World,* Clark W. Bryan of *Good Housekeeping,* and Horace Elisha Scudder of the *Atlantic Monthly*—so deeply had Bellamy penetrated the field of popular discussion in America. From every area of thought and activity, he attracted youthful devotees, among them John Dewey in philosophy and education, William Allen White in journalism, Eugene V. Debs in labor, Walter Rauschenbusch in religion, and Thorstein Veblen in economics and social psychology; and through these men, each to become a seminal figure in his special field, Bellamy profoundly influenced the American mind.

However, one religious reviewer took Bellamy to task for the material qualities of his utopia. Reminding Bellamy that "Jesus was a peasant with nowhere to lay his head," the reviewer urged a religious disregard for environment, concluding, "It is certainly a new idea in the world that virtue is the child of comfort." To such criticisms, Bellamy replied that spiritual problems could not be separated from material ones, that religion, in fact, waited on economic reform. In "To A Pastor," Bellamy said: "The reorganization of society which is needed to render Christianity possible is an industrial and economic reorganization. . . . do not delude yourself with the idea that any amount of moral reformation can solve a problem which in basis is essentially economic. . . . [First] clear away obstacles which have hitherto hindered the progress of Christianity and [you] will open to it a career such as the imagination of a saint never pictured. The trouble with the present competitive system of business is that it will not let a man be good, though he wants to." [1]

Another frequently expressed religious criticism of Bellamy was that his system, designed to eradicate poverty, opposed Jesus' observation, "The poor ye have always with you." The

[1] See pp. 134-137.

acceptance of this statement as prophecy angered Bellamy. In an age that gave birth to the Higher Criticism, Bellamy was able to interpret this statement along new, positive lines: "Somewhere else I believe Christ tells his disciples that two duties sum up all the law and the prophets: one being to love God wholly, the other to love one's neighbor as one's self. Now, how long do you think, if everybody loved his neighbor as himself, there would be left any who were poorer than his neighbors? . . . if there is any such thing as blasphemy it surely consists in quoting the great apostle of human brotherhood against the abolition of poverty." [2]

Bellamy felt strongly about Christ's role in social history. In his notes are several fragments referring to Jesus as a divine social reformer: "Jesus Christ . . . a man seeking to wipe away tears and to succor those in need. . . . To suppose Christ God would be to detract from his glory, would be to hold him responsible for the woes of humanity which, far from being responsible for, he tried his best to cure" (Notebook B, pp. 4-5).

Determined to see the birth of a nobler social order, and encouraged by the success of his book to think people ready for it, Bellamy began a crusade for "Nationalism," the name he gave to the social system outlined in his utopia. He attracted such supporters as William Dean Howells, "the Dean of American Letters"; Thomas Wentworth Higginson, colonel of the first colored regiment in the Civil War; General Arthur F. Devereaux, "the hero of Gettysburg"; the Reverend Edward Everett Hale, author of *The Man Without A Country;* and Julia Ward Howe, author of "The Battle-Hymn of the Republic."

Devoting his time, money, and health to the cause, Bellamy lectured and wrote extensively, often referring to "Nationalism" as "a religion," "a Judgment Day," or "God's kingdom of fraternal equality." In the Social Gospel movement, Bellamy saw an auspicious sign for the early triumph of social ethics: "One of the most hopeful features of the Nationalist

2 *Talks on Nationalism,* pp. 65-66.

outlook from the first has been the heartiness with which a large contingent of the clergy has enlisted in it, claiming that it was, as it truly is, nothing more than Christianity applied to industrial organization. This we hope to make so apparent that ere long all Christian men shall be obliged either to abjure Christ or come with us." [3]

While it is true, as Bellamy said, that he received enthusiastic support and encouragement from social gospelers, both clerical and lay, the movement, though articulate and colorful, was still small (see May, p. 196), and unable to lend much support. Social gospelers were meeting increasing resistance to their thinking. George D. Herron, leading social gospeler of the nineties, after delivering a commencement address at the University of Nebraska, sat on the platform to hear himself scathingly attacked as an anarchist by the governor of the state. And, in public dramatization of the split among churchmen over the Social Gospel, of the nine ministers on the platform, "two doctors divine made haste to shake hands with the governor; four slipped away quickly; and three came to Dr. Herron with hearts greatly stirred and grasped his hand" (Dombrowski, p. 178). The "Three Earthquakes" unloosed by the violent strikes of 1877, 1886, and 1892-94 had not yet altered Protestant conservatism (See May, p. 91), although Bellamy's Nationalist Movement seemed to enjoy a good deal of success in the propagation of its ideas.[4] Finally, poor in health and depleted in funds, Bellamy withdrew from politics.

He retired from the political arena with his earlier opinions on religion and the church even more strongly confirmed. Paul, the author's son, recalls his father reading from the Scriptures in the last few years of his life: "He commented as he read, and always emphasized the social and humanistic side of the teachings of Jesus. He used to tell us how he was quite sure that the all-important thing was how we treated

[3] *Edward Bellamy Speaks Again!* pp. 139-140.
[4] See John Hope Franklin, "Edward Bellamy and the Nationalist Movement," *New England Quarterly*, XI (Dec. 1938), 739-772.

our fellow men. . . . He said that the reason he did not want us to go to church was because he felt the church failed to put the emphasis on religion where it belonged, namely on the translation of the Golden Rule into human relations; that it sang constantly about the glories of Heaven and did not denounce or attempt to correct evil and wickedness here below." [5] Unfortunately, Bellamy did not live long enough to see the Social Gospel receive official Protestant church blessing in the organization of the Federal Council of the Churches of Christ in America,[6] just ten years after his death in 1898.

IX

Bellamy's influence, both at home and abroad, continues to be incalculable. Depressions, insecurity, and war have spurred the recollection of his utopianism as a form of counter-assertion. He is appreciatively discussed in many biographies, forums, textbooks in literature, history, architecture, education, and philosophy, in countless masters' and doctoral theses, even in a detective story; and *Looking Backward* still appears in at least four plentiful editions in the United States, one publisher alone having reprinted 100,000 copies in 1945.

Contemporary observers recognize in Bellamy an accurate prophet of present forms of social welfare, industrial organization, and mechanical invention (e. g., the electric eye, radio, and television). His genius for prophecy appears to be rooted in sympathetic awareness of the profound human desire for economic security and personal dignity. That such a desire is the key to American development was emphasized by a distinguished committee of the American Historical Association chaired by Charles A. Beard.[1] Further, an informed observer,

[5] In Arthur E. Morgan, *The Philosophy of Edward Bellamy* (New York, 1945), pp. 84-85.

[6] See Charles Hopkins, *The Rise of the Social Gospel in American Protestantism* (New Haven, 1940), pp. 280-317.

[1] See "The Climate of American Ideas," Report of the Commission on the Social Studies, Part I (New York, 1932), pp. 79-81.

looking back from the vantage point of 1954, could aptly say of Bellamy: "he caught hold of the wave of the future long before it broke upon the shore." [2]

It is likely that of all his remarkable insights, future developments will highlight his insistence upon the reality of co-operative factors. In an age obsessed with Malthusian-Darwinian-Spencerian images of the struggle for survival, Bellamy sketched a co-operative commonwealth and ably defended it as harmonious with man's needs and desires. In the storm of criticism that greeted his faith in man's goodness, he insisted: "There is no stronger attribute of human nature than this hunger for comradeship and mutual trust." [3] Today, scientists in many fields have produced evidence that validates Bellamy's lofty view.[4]

However, several contemporary critics have asserted that Bellamy was egregiously mistaken in his views. Current fears of enveloping totalitarianism have evoked laments, mingled with jeers, for Bellamy's nationalization of industry, conscription of labor, and boundless trust in the managerial elite.[5] Certainly, Bellamy's enchantment with vast combines on grounds of pure efficiency seems soulless to urban people sick for want of face-to-face relationships.

Above all, Bellamy's concept of a society in perfect equilibrium, with little need for further innovation or fresh thinking, is a chimera, since all human endeavor (as distinct from animal and insect life) is characterized by conscious change. But, in fairness to Edward Bellamy, it must be added that his vision of the future did not find full expression in *Looking Backward*. "A whole infinity" of human development stretched beyond it, but he had only outlined this when death came to him at the age of forty-eight.

---

2 George J. Becker, "Edward Bellamy: Utopia, American Plan," *Antioch Review*, XIV (Summer, 1954), 193.

3 *Talks on Nationalism*, p. 101.

4 See Ashley Montagu, *On Being Human* (New York, 1950) and *Darwin: Competition and Cooperation* (New York, 1952).

5 See, for example, Marie Louise Berneri, *Journey Through Utopia* (Boston, 1950), pp. 243-255.

Yet, approaches to Bellamy flowing from twentieth-century currents misinterpret his spirit and purpose. One must re-create the author's time in order to understand his genesis. Bellamy began his writing career in the seventies, a period of crass materialism justly lampooned in *The Gilded Age* (1873) by Mark Twain and Charles Dudley Warner. With more earnestness, Henry George identified the central prob-lem of the age in the title of his classic, *Progress and Poverty* (1879), sharply outlining the disconcerting relationship be-tween growing wealth and growing want. Many other writers in America began to feel the urgency of this quandary, among them Walt Whitman, Sidney Lanier, and Howells.

In Bellamy's lifetime the problem of progress and poverty assumed far-embracing proportions disturbing to every thoughtful person. Pope Leo XIII in his historic encyclical, *The Condition of Labor* (1891), warned the world:

The momentous seriousness of the present state of things just now fills every mind with painful apprehension; wise men discuss it; practical men propose schemes; popular meet-ings, legislatures, and sovereign princes, all are occupied with it—and there is nothing which has a deeper hold on public attention. . . . all agree, and there can be no question what-ever, that some remedy must be found, and quickly found, for the misery and wretchedness which press so heavily at this moment on the large majority of the very poor . . . given over, isolated and defenseless, to the callousness of employers, and the greed of unrestrained competition . . . a yoke little better than slavery itself.[6]

It is to Bellamy's everlasting credit that he (along with many others) addressed himself to devising one possible solu-tion to the problem of progress and poverty, producing the most influential novel in America since *Uncle Tom's Cabin* (1852). Endeavoring to build "a City of God, to shame . . . the imperfections of the City of Man,"[7] he limned a social

[6] From the official translation, reprinted in Henry George, *The Land Question* (Garden City, 1891), pp. 109-111.

[7] From Irwin Edman's Introduction to *Looking Backward* (Hollywood, 1941), Limited Editions Club.

order of welfare programs, garden cities and public works, mechanization of labor, vast educational resources, women freed of household drudgery—recognizable features, in great measure, of contemporary industrial society—and, greatest blessing of all (this still to be achieved), people living together as loving brothers.

Although Henry George, expressing a widely held opinion, dismissed *Looking Backward* as "a castle in the air with clouds for its foundation," actually the materials for Bellamy's "Golden Age" can be found in characteristic developments of his time, as, for example: the pioneering role in America of his own native Massachusetts in free public schools, in public health (with the establishment of the first state department of public health, 1869), in factory legislation (with the adoption of the "Ten Hour Act for Women and Children," 1874); the imaginative landscaping of Central Park by Frederick Olmsted; the inventions of Edison and Bell; the emergence of women both at home and abroad as an articulate political force; British municipalities offering many services of a personal type (such as public bathhouses and reading rooms); the inauguration of public controls over private industry in Australia, notably in wages and hours; and, particularly, the stunning rise to power of Bismarckian Germany through universal military service and social insurance. Intending *Looking Backward* "as a forecast, in accordance with the principles of evolution," Bellamy allowed his rich imagination full play with such phenomena.

Despite shifts in critical evaluations of Bellamy's role and status, he remains what he has always been for millions of readers, a social evangelist. His eloquent insistence upon society's collective responsibility for each individual's welfare inspired the *New York Times* to comment editorially upon Bellamy's centenary in 1950: ". . . he was able to persuade other men to look at the evils of the world and . . . to hope that some day they might be eradicated, to work to find some program for their eradication, and not to accept with smugness any belief that a world where children can starve and stunt could be the best of all possible worlds. Therein, and not in any specific program, lay his greatest influence." [8] To Bellamy, the American dream of the brave new world, the holy commonwealth, the land of the free, the melting pot, the good neighbor was all so real that he exalted it into a religion.

Does not this influence move with the mainstream of history? Arnold J. Toynbee, in his celebrated *A Study of History* (Vols. VII to X, 1954), insists that the only solution to the riddle of pain is for men to learn to revere each other in the realization that God is love.

Bellamy himself touched upon this very problem in a newspaper editorial years ago:

Reformations cannot go on long by force of antagonisms to wrongs in society. Hate power may start a crusade against moral evil but will not keep it up. The world is set right by love, and this demands confidence in goodness and trust in God. Positive forces are the . . . clear, strong, mighty beliefs in the good time coming, and in the power of Christian truth and grace to bring it about. The doubters and deniers cannot march in the van of this army.[9]

X

In his final book, *Equality,*[1] doggedly written under the shadow of death, Bellamy gave his religious-social philosophy final, definitive shape. To Bellamy, religion was an active, ethical principle of love, operating in the world as the solvent of man's cares and conflicts. In *Equality,* the Reverend Mr. Barton, Bellamy's spiritual spokesman, outlines religion as it is practiced in the "Republic of the Golden Rule." It has become completely "modern," yet thoroughly faithful to its historic origins. There are few, if any, churches. Instead, ministers preach over the telephone and electroscope (television) to huge audiences. Mechanical improvements and new attitudes toward the practice of religion have rendered church

8 March 25, 1950, p. 12.

9 "Touching Things Spiritual," *Springfield Daily Union,* Nov. 27, 1875, p. 4.

1 See pp. 27-44, 77-79, 124-128.

worship obsolete. The clergy, drastically reduced in number because of the power of one preacher to reach thousands, provides a "leadership of moral and intellectual genius" to a people who have long since outgrown the "ceremonial side of religion . . . [which] meant so much in the child-time of the race." The Reverend Mr. Barton proudly announces that in reaching such a point, the citizens of utopia have fulfilled a prophecy of Jesus: "The time has now fully come which Christ foretold in that talk with the woman by the well of Samaria when the idea of the Temple and all it stood for would give place to the wholly spiritual religion, without respect of times or places, which he declared most pleasing to God." [2]

One of the happiest aspects of utopian religion is the complete absence of sects and creeds. These artificial barriers between men "were completely swept away and forgotten in the passionate impulse of brotherly love which brought men together for the founding of a nobler social order." The disappearance of "church organization and machinery," and "sectarian demarcations and doctrinal differences," were signals for "the beginning of a world-awakening of impassioned interest in the vast concerns covered by the word religion." [3]

Bellamy's strongest motives were religious. Convinced that man had within him seeds of the divine, he believed these could flower only in favorable social soil. A lifelong friend and fellow social gospeler, the Reverend R. F. Bisbee, asked Bellamy about the ultimate social aim of his writings, and reported the following conversation: " 'Mr. Bellamy, you do not consider the social state pictured in *Equality* the end of human progress, do you?' 'Oh, no,' he replied with what I felt to be almost a touch of impatience: 'it is only the beginning. When we get there we shall find a whole infinity beyond.' These were his last words to me. . . . There he stood, that little pale man, within eight months of his death, with a faraway look in his eyes which I shall never forget, as he repeated—'A whole infinity beyond.' " [4]

2 See p. 32.   3 See pp. 34ff.

4 In Morgan, *Edward Bellamy*, p. 420.

CHRONOLOGY

1850 Born March 26 into the family of a Baptist minister in Chicopee Falls, Massachusetts, a village in process of becoming a mill town.

1867 Failed the physical requirements for admission to West Point. Disconsolate, took a course in literature at Union College, where his brother Frederick was a student.

1868–69 Spent several months traveling in Europe, and living in Dresden, Germany, as a companion to his wealthy cousin, William Packer, of Brooklyn.

 In Europe, he became aware of "man's inhumanity to man." Upon his return home, in 1869, undertook the study of law in the firm of Leonard and Wells of Springfield, Massachusetts.

1871 Admitted to the Massachusetts bar, but abandoned law as a career after taking one case.

1871–72 Served on the editorial staff of the *New York Evening Post*.

 Delivered an address on "The Barbarism of Society" before the Chicopee Falls Village Lyceum.

1872 In June, returned to Springfield as book reviewer and editorial writer for the *Springfield Daily Union*.

 Began writing short stories which were eventually published in several of the leading literary magazines of the day.

1873 "The Panic of 1873," world-wide in scope, brought hard times to the Springfield area, including Chicopee.

1874 Wrote "The Religion of Solidarity," which he called the "germ" of his philosophy, but never offered it for publication.

1877 Because of poor health, gave up newspaper work to visit Hawaii with his brother Frederick.

1878 Anonymously published *Six to One: A Nantucket Idyl.*

 Undertook the simultaneous writing of two novels to be published in serialized form, *Dr. Heidenhoff's Process*, dealing with the guilt complex, for the *Springfield Union*, and *The Duke of Stockbridge: A Romance of Shays' Rebellion* for the *Berkshire Courier*.

1880   Established the tri-weekly *Penny News* (soon renamed the *Springfield Daily News*) with his brother Charles.

1881   Left the newspaper world to return to free-lance writing.

1882   Married Emma Augusta Sanderson, who had lived with his family as a legal ward for eight years. His father, the Reverend Rufus Bellamy, forced to resign as minister of the Central Baptist Church of Chicopee for unascertainable reasons.
        Withdrew from church membership.

1884   *Miss Ludington's Sister: A Romance of Immortality* published.
        His first child, Paul, born.

1886   His daughter Marion born.
        Against the background of Haymarket and "ten thousand strikes," began work on *Looking Backward: 2000–1887,* "a fairy tale of social felicity," which transformed itself into a "vehicle of industrial reorganization."

1888   *Looking Backward* published in January.
        The First Nationalist Club of Boston, established in December, began to organize public opinion in support of Bellamy's social thought.

1889   By December, *Looking Backward,* selling ten thousand copies a week, had reached the two hundred thousand mark. One of the most widely discussed books of the century, it was soon to be translated into many foreign languages.

1891   Bellamy founded his own weekly, *The New Nation,* with himself as editor, "to educate the public" towards bringing about "an industrial system based upon the principles of human brotherhood."

1894   Suffering chronic ill-health and limited in finances, he forsook political journalism to work on *Equality,* a sequel to *Looking Backward.*

1897   Plagued by tuberculosis, Bellamy visited Denver in search of a cure.
        Equality, his final work, published.

1898   Died May 22 in Chicopee Falls, at the age of forty-eight, of pharyngeal tuberculosis and possible cancer of the throat. Buried in Chicopee.

SELECTED BIBLIOGRAPHY

The Author's Writings

Six to One: A Nantucket Idyl. New York, 1878 (published anonymously).

Dr. Heidenhoff's Process. New York, 1880.

Miss Ludington's Sister: A Romance of Immortality. Boston, 1884.

Looking Backward: 2000–1887. Boston, 1888.

Equality. New York, 1897.

The Blindman's World and Other Stories. Boston, 1898.

The Duke of Stockbridge: A Romance of Shays' Rebellion. New York, 1900.

Edward Bellamy Speaks Again! Articles, Public Addresses, Letters. Kansas City, 1937.

Talks on Nationalism. Chicago, 1938.

The Religion of Solidarity. Yellow Springs, Ohio, 1940. Edited by Arthur E. Morgan.

The Bellamy Collection. Available in the Houghton Library, Harvard University (includes Bellamy's Notebooks, Journals, and Correspondence, as well as material about him).

Edward Bellamy's Book Reviews and Editorials. Identified and copied in manuscript by Mrs. Marion Bellamy Earnshaw and Bellamy Earnshaw of Springfield, Massachusetts.

Collateral Reading

Aaron, Daniel, *Men of Good Hope.* New York, 1951.

Becker, George J., "Edward Bellamy: Utopia, American Plan," *Antioch Review,* XIV, 181-194, Summer, 1954.

Berneri, Marie Louise, *Journey Through Utopia.* Boston, 1950.

Curti, Merle, Shryock, R. H., Cochran, T. C., and Harrington, F. H., *American History.* 2 vols. New York, 1950.

Dombrowski, James, *The Early Days of Christian Socialism in America*. New York, 1936.

Filler, Louis, "Edward Bellamy and the Spiritual Unrest," *The American Journal of Economics and Sociology*, VIII, 239-249, Apr., 1949.

Franklin, John Hope, "Edward Bellamy and the Nationalist Movement," *The New England Quarterly*, XI, 739-772, Dec., 1938.

Hertzler, Joyce Oramel, *The History of Utopian Thought*. New York, 1926.

May, Henry F., *Protestant Churches and Industrial America*, New York, 1949.

Morgan, Arthur E., *Edward Bellamy*. New York, 1944.

———, *The Philosophy of Edward Bellamy*. New York, 1945.

Parkes, Henry Bamford, *The American Experience*. New York, 1947.

Parrington, Vernon L., *Main Currents in American Thought*. 3 vols. New York, 1930.

Parrington, Vernon L., Jr., *American Dreams: A Study of American Utopias*. Providence, 1947.

Sadler, Elizabeth, "One Book's Influence: Edward Bellamy's *Looking Backward*," *The New England Quarterly*, XVII, 530-555, Dec., 1944.

Schiffman, Joseph, "Edward Bellamy's Altruistic Man," *American Quarterly*, VI, 195-209, Fall, 1954.

———, "Edward Bellamy's Religious Thought," *PMLA* (*Publications of the Modern Language Association of America*), LXVIII, 716-732, Sept., 1953.

Shurter, Robert L., "The Writing of *Looking Backward*," *The South Atlantic Quarterly*, XXXVIII, 255-261, July, 1939.

Taylor, Walter Fuller, *The Economic Novel in America*. Chapel Hill, 1942.

NOTE ON THE TEXT

The present edition attempts to present for the first time a cross section of Edward Bellamy's varied writings. The selections have been organized under four main headings, each expressing a characteristic Bellamy theme. Titles for almost all these selections have been supplied by the editor, and they appear in brackets.

The editor has taken the liberty of modernizing Bellamy's spelling, and of occasionally changing his punctuation and grammar, in the interests of readability.

Only one of Bellamy's works, the frequently reprinted *Looking Backward,* presented the opportunity (and the problem) of a choice of text. From among the many available editions of this novel, the editor chose to reprint parts of The Riverside Press edition of Houghton Mifflin (Boston, 1941). However, in instances of obvious misprints, misspellings, and errors of omission in that text, the editor resorted to a much earlier printing, the June 16, 1888 edition of Ticknor & Company of Boston (Number 38 Extra in Ticknor's Paper Series).

All of Bellamy's other works are out of print, and several are impossible to obtain, except through a few libraries.

EDWARD BELLAMY
SELECTED WRITINGS ON
RELIGION AND SOCIETY

I. THE RELIGION OF SOLIDARITY

THE RELIGION OF SOLIDARITY [1]

The emotions of pleasurable melancholy and of wistful yearning produced by the prospect of a beautiful landscape are matters of universal experience, a commonplace of poetry. Upon analysis this mental experience seems to consist, if we may so express it, in a vague desire to enter into, to possess, and be a part of the beauty before the eye, to come into some closer union with it than is possible consistently with the conditions of our natures. This subdued, yet intense attraction, in its disappointment produces an indefinable sadness, and it is thus that is to be explained, at least in large part, the melancholy so often observed to result from the contemplation of natural beauty. It is the disappointment of the desire after a more perfect communion. There are times in the experience of most persons of emotional temperament in which this desire (I had almost called it lust) after natural beauty amounts to a veritable orgasm. How often in the brooding warmth and stillness of summer nights, when the senses are fairly oppressed with natural beauty, and the perfumed air is laden with voluptuous solicitations, does the charm of nature grow so intense that it seems almost personal, and under its influence the senses are sublimed to an ecstasy. It is then that some almost palpable barrier seems to hold back the soul from merging with the being toward which it so passionately tends.

Sometimes with the storm wind, with moonlit waters, with wooded glens and purling brooks, with the solitary soul of

[1] [Reprinted by permission of Arthur E. Morgan.]

3

mid-ocean, with lovely mountaintops, with the sunset eternally glowing over the rim of the rolling earth, with the dewy freshness of the ever-virginal morning, with the new and tender pulse of spring, the thronging life, the voluptuous languor of summer, the restfulness of autumn; with these all and other innumerable aspects of nature, the human spirit sympathizes; and in this communion, despite the tinge of melancholy resulting from its imperfect consummation, finds one of its chiefest consolations and asylums.

Thus continually does the spirit in man betray affinity with nature by vague and seemingly purposeless longings to attain a more perfect sympathy with it. So far as this universal and strongly marked instinct can be distinctly interpreted, it indicates in human nature some element common with external nature, toward which it is attracted, as with the attraction of a part toward a whole, and with a violence that oftentimes renders us painfully conscious of the rigorous confines of our individual organisms. This restless and discontented element is not at home in the personality, its union with it seems mechanical rather than chemical, rather of position than of essence. It is homesick for a vaster mansion than the personality affords, with an unconquerable yearning, a divine discontent tending elsewhither.

The emotion induced in us by the monuments of bygone life are of the sort that rebel against the conditions of our organisms as persons. How often has it happened to each and every one of us to stand before some such monument of old life, some ruined specimen of ancient handiwork, some dead city or deserted site. The place is associated with the lives of generations long since moldered away, and the gentle ghosts of their joys and sorrows seem to hover around the familiar spot, bathing it in a haze of vague reminiscence. We are conscious of a sense of loss, a feeling of deprivation, at having had no part in the skein of life that once raveled and tangled on this very spot. We are conscious of a repining at the barrier of time that has included and shut us up in today.

The experience is very similar when, as we muse earnestly

on the glories of future ages, the vision of the world to be rises before us, and we feel that in essence we belong no more to today than to yesterday and tomorrow. Such limitations appear to be arbitrary and irrelevant, impertinent though impregnable. Hungry, not for more life, but for all the life there is, we count ourselves robbed of the days when we were not and those in which we shall not be. The reader of history surveys past ages with their processions of heroes and grand dramas, as one looks upon a wide and varied country from a mountaintop. What a painful incongruity is he conscious of between the soul, so easily contemporary with all time, and like an unseen presence mingling with the doings and strivings of ancient man, and his individuality weighted down to a little point of time. How trifling seems that point compared with the vast expanse seen from it, as seems his standpoint to the rapt watcher on the mountain brow, whose gaze walks unimpeded up and down the streets of a hundred villages, and follows, unfelt, the steps of the toilers in a thousand widely parted fields. The mind is conscious of a discontent that would be indignation but for its conscious impotence, that it should be thus unequal to itself. It has the aspirations of a god with the limitations of a clod, a soul that seeks to enfold and animate the universe, that takes all being for its province, and, with such potential compass and desire, has for its sole task the animating of one human animal in a corner of an insignificant planet.

Now who can doubt that the human soul has more in common with that life of all time and all things toward which it so eagerly goes out, than with that narrow, isolated, and incommodious individuality, the thrall of time and space, to which it so reluctantly, and with such a sense of belittlement and degradation, perforce returns.

Mysterious and likewise taking hold on infinite things are the emotions excited by the weird music of the Aeolian harp or the soughing of the wind in a pine forest. The music is so low, so fine, and so far-off, that we seem to hear it by some inner ear, and we listen in involuntary awe as to the still small voice of nature. There is a sound as if the tones came from the far-off places of the universe; they intimate vast solitudes, wideness, boundless enlargement, eternal calm, eternal rhythm. In that whispered infinitude we would repose as in our proper medium; in that voice we strive to voice ourselves. We strain after the fuller life of which we recognize the sound but cannot comprehend the reality. In such moments we reach out of one plane of existence into another, and then sink back as sinks a swimmer, with grasping hands and despairing eyes turned toward the empyrean vault.

Very often in like manner must it happen to everyone, when wandering abroad at night, to feel the eyes drawn upward as by a sense of majestic, overshadowing presence. We gaze into the bottomless star-measured depths of the skies, whose infinite profounds are for the moment curtained by no cloud. The soul of the gazer is drawn through the eyes; and on and on, from star to star, still travels toward infinity. He is strange to the limitations of terrestrial things; he is out of the body. He is oppressed with the grandeur of the universal frame; its weight seems momentarily to rest upon his shoulders. But with a start and a wrench as of life from soul the personality reasserts itself; he awakes to himself, and with a temporary sense of strangeness fits himself once again to the pygmy standards about him.

The experiences which have been mentioned are but examples of the sublime, ecstatic, impersonal emotions, transcending the scope of personality or individuality, manifested by human nature, and of which the daily life of every person affords abundant instances. What, then, is the view of human nature thus suggested? Truly, one strange and awesome. On the one hand is the personal life, an atom, a grain of sand on a boundless shore, a bubble on a foam-flecked ocean, a life bearing a proportion to the mass of past, present, and future life so infinitesimal as to defy the imagination. Such is the importance of the person. On the other hand is a certain other life, as it were a spark of the universal life, insatiable in aspiration, greedy of infinity, asserting solidarity with all things and all existence, containing the limitations of space and time and all other of the restricting conditions of the personality. On the one hand is a little group of faculties of the individual, unable even to cope with the few and simple conditions of material life, wretchedly failing, for the most part, to secure tolerable satisfaction for the physical needs of the race, and at best making slow and painful progression. On the other hand, in the soul, is a depth of divine despair over the insufficiency of this existence, already seemingly too large, and a passionate dream of immortality, the vision of a starving man whose fancy revels in full tables. Such is the estate of man, and such his dual life. As an individual he finds it a task exceeding his powers even to secure satisfactory material conditions for his physical life; as a universal he grasps at a life infinitely larger than the one he so poorly cares for. This dual life of man, personal and impersonal, as an individual and as a universal, goes far to explain the riddle of human nature and human destiny. . . .[2]

Since it is a common error to imagine the impersonal consciousness as a thing altogether vague and shadowy, while the personal consciousness or soul life is the only real and substantial hold on existence, it will be well by way of correcting this notion to advert to some of the continual instances in our daily spiritual experience in which we closely approximate the impersonal mood. For instance, in the degree in which we realize beauty of any sort we approach the impersonal condition and obtain a hint of the mode of our impersonal consciousness. It is only when we can say that we forget ourselves and in a certain mystic way seem to share the life of the thing admired that we taste the pure and high felicity of a perfect realization of a perfect sense of beauty. It is in measure as we are wrapt out of ourselves into this mood of impersonal consciousness that we are sublimed by the impulses of self-devotion and attain the grand experience of enthusiasm. Those mental states which we call the noblest, broadest, and

[2] [Here several pages of the manuscript seem to be missing.]

most inspired, the most intense and satisfying of our psychical felicities, in fine all those emotions and moods by which we are greater than our personalities, and which constitute the larger and far more essential part of our lives—all these are but the activity of the greater self, the impersonal consciousness within us.

The fact of consciousness most clearly witnessing to the impersonality of the soul is that whereas the animal functions are constant quantities, varying only with their supplies of nutriment and stimulus, the soul is most inconstant, as if it were continually coming and going, now dull and lifeless, now again vivified, glowing, expanding as it is touched with some inspiration of enthusiasm or some sentiment of sympathy with the larger life. I know of nothing with which to compare this continual flux and reflux but to the phenomena presented by the Northern Lights, which on a winter night now irradiate the whole vault of the heavens with torrents of light, throwing their spray over the earth, and again sinking away to the horizon, leaving the sky black and dead. So is the soul, ever rising and falling, wavering, undulating, ever glowing and fading, ebbing and flowing, as from some eternal reservoir. "The wind bloweth where it listeth, and thou hearest the sound thereof, but canst not tell whence it cometh, and whither it goeth." So is the soul of man born again in every fresh inbreathing of the soul of solidarity.

In view of such phenomena, where is the claim of the personality of the soul, and its sufficient, self-comprehending consciousness? I can as easily imagine the little inlets of the ocean coast boasting that the tides that daily throb through them are spontaneous with them, as a man boasting that these tides and tempests of the soul arise within his own personality, and do not rather come from the uttermost parts of the universe.

Genius is the vivid partaking of the soul of solidarity. It is essentially impersonal in its manifestations; the personality of the subject is in suspense. To be possessed of his genius, the man must be unconscious of his personality; he must be beside himself, even as the Delphic priestess was required to be before the oracle spoke through her. We can but conclude, then, from all this testimony of our own experiences, that unconsciousness of personality or impersonal consciousness does not imply a vague and shadowy mode of being, but rather a stronger, intenser pulse of feeling than is obtainable in the most vigorous assertion of the personality. Individuality, personality, partiality, is segregation, is partition, is confinement; is, in fine, a prison, and happy are we if its walls grow not wearisome ere our seventy years' sentence expires.

To pursue this argument, it appears to me (the testimony of his own consciousness is the only evidence that any person can receive in this matter) that the last effort in introspection discloses in the penetralia of the soul an impersonal consciousness. Tracing to its awful source the river of life within us, what do we find it, we who claim so confidently to be personal, self-comprehending, self-complete entities? Will anyone be so bold as to say that he can fathom, even in untranslatable emotions, that fount of being whence wells the sense of existence? Ponder well. Do we not feel ourselves at once a part of, and external to, the last impregnable consciousness, that citadel of being? We are at once it and of it, itself, yet not all of it. In fine, it is impersonal. It is the witness of our life, and we are the witness of its life. With nothing are we more identical, yet it is as awful to us as infinity, unspeakable as God. Ask for no heavens to open nor firmament to dissolve that you may be left faced with God and see the sum end of things. Steadfastly look into the well of your own life and know the powerlessness of human tongues to express its endless depths, its boundless contents. Ere you think of any other infinity, fathom and compass that, and be prepared to learn that there is but one problem in the universe, and that is the nature of the soul, which is one in you and in all things.

Moods of insight visit us all, in which our natures go deepening on and up, until we feel we are infinity within ourselves and turn back shuddering from its brink. The pettiness of the personality comes in sharp contrast with these stupendous and labyrinthine reaches of the soul, forming a bizarre and glaring opposition, seeming inscrutable, and impressing us with a strange sense of mystery and self-ignorance. But when we come to regard the profound within us as the presence of the All of being, with which we are far more deeply and indissolubly identical than with our individualities, to which the contrasted pettinesses pertain, we cease to mingle the two strains of emotions but act in one and rest in the other.

There are few of an introspective habit who are not haunted with a certain very definite sense of a second soul, an inner serene and passionless ego, which regards the experiences of the individual with a superior curiosity, as it were, a half-pity. It is especially in moments of the deepest anguish or of the maddest gaiety, that is, in the intensest strain of the individuality, that we are conscious of the dual soul as of a presence serenely regarding from another plane of being the agitated personality. It is at such times that we become, not by force of argument, but by spontaneous experience, strictly subjective to ourselves, that is, the individuality becomes objective to the universal soul, that eternal subjective. The latter regards the former as a god is conceived to look upon man, in an attitude passionless, disinterested, yet pitiful. Often does it happen in scenes of revelry or woe that we are thus suddenly translated, looking down calmly upon our passion-wrung selves, and then, as with an effort, once more enduring the weeds or tinsel of our personal estates. At such times we say that we have been out of ourselves, but in reality we have been into ourselves; we have only just realized the greater half of our being. We have momentarily lived in the infinite part of our being, a region ever open and waiting for us if we will but frequent its highlands. We call such an experience abnormal; it should be normal.

We dwell needlessly in the narrow grotto of the individual life, counting as strange, angelic visitants the sunbeams that struggle thither, not being able to believe that the upper universe is our world to live in, the grotto of the personality a mere workshop. We are content to conjecture from occasional intuitions a world that we should constantly recognize. The half-conscious god that is man is called to recognize his divine parts. The soul then is what it would be. It has the infinity it craves. We restrict ourselves.

Spread your wings; you will reach no horizon. Cast out the lead; it will strike no bottom. Our little wells are filled from this eternal life; our souls are not islands in the void, but peninsulas forming one continent of life within the universe. It is man's own indolence that will inhabit but one corner of the open universe, a corner of himself. Let him assume his birthright, and live out, live up, in others, in the past, in the future, in nature, in God. There are no barriers to the soul but such as sense-bound fancy imagines. When Thales enunciated the maxim "Know thyself," he propounded a problem not to be solved, for the human soul is continuous with it. The dual existence of man is at once infinite and infinitesimal and particular.

I do not assert that the higher universal life is at once realizable by merely resolving thereon. Like his present endowment of mental faculties which man has slowly and painfully evolved since the savage state, so the full consciousness and active enjoyment of the universal soul will be slow and difficult in being realized. Potentially, indeed, the universal life is manifesting itself within us by countless unmistakable signs, but it is in the mind of Shakespeare as in the cave-dweller's. It remains for us, by culture of our spiritual cognitions, by education, drawing forth of our partially latent universal instincts, to develop into a consciousness as coherent, definite, and indefeasible as that of our individual life, the all-identical life of the universe within us. Nor is this tendency of the human soul to a more perfect realization of its solidarity with the universe, by the development of instincts partly or wholly latent, altogether a theory. It is already an observed fact, a matter of history. I would call attention to the fact that sentimental love of the beautiful and sublime in nature, the charm which mountains, sea, and landscape so potently exercise upon the modern mind through a subtle sense of sympathy, is a comparatively modern and recent growth of the human mind. The ancients knew, or at least say, nothing of it. It is a curious fact that in no classical author are to be found any allusions to a class of emotions and sentiments that take up such large space in modern literature. It is almost within a century, in fact, that this susceptibility of the soul seems to have been developed. It is therefore not surprising that its language should still be vague. I am sure that much of the unrest and reaching out after the infinite, which is the peculiar characteristic of this age, is the result of this new sense. If culture can add such a province as this to human nature within a century, it is surely not visionary to count on a still more complete future development of the same group of subtle psychical faculties.

The influence of an acceptance of the view of life which has now been outlined should not be to breed a discontent with ourselves as individuals. The personality should not be contemned, should not be worn with half-heartedness and repining. It is dignified in being the channel, the expression of the universal. In this view it has as sound a right of being as the universal itself. Its joys we do well to push to the uttermost, interpreting them by the universal and thus lending them sublimity. Its sorrows we should not, on the other hand, contemn nor bear too heavily, but tenderly pity from the higher plane the bereavements of the individual, accepting their monitions toward the universal, the all-pervading life. In that lofty, overlooking region, in that supernal, passionless atmosphere, learn to make a home and build there an everlasting habitation, whither to retire when the personal life is overclouded, its windows darkened, and all its functions palsied with the bitterness of disappointment and the anguish of bereavement.

Perhaps the relations of the universal and individual lives may be more distinctly brought before the mind by imagining them under the types, respectively, of the centripetal and centrifugal forces as illustrated in celestial mechanics. The instinct of universal solidarity, of the identity of our lives with all life, is the centripetal force which binds together in certain orbits all orders of beings. In fine, the instinct of solidarity in the moral universe correlates with the attraction of gravitation in the material world.

The fact of individuality with its tendency to particularizations is the centrifugal force which hinders the universal fusion, the natural result of the unimpeded operation of the centripetal force, and preserves the variety in unity which seems the destined condition of being. Thus these mutually balancing forces play each its necessary part, and each we may suppose to be an absolute fact. It is the instinct of personality which leads man, weary of exploring the universe and striving to grasp the relations of it to other orders of being, to take refuge in the bundle of mental and physical experiences which he calls himself, as the only thing of which he is absolutely sure, the sole rock in the midst of an illimitable ocean. It is this instinct which at times sends him off, as it were, on a tangent from his orbit, in defiance of the centripetal instinct of solidarity, in mad self-assertion, in wild rebellion against subordination or coherency with anything.

It is this vicious habit of regarding the personality as an ultimate fact instead of a mere temporary affection of the universal that at times overcomes the mind with a sense of utter and unnecessary isolation, of inexpressible loneliness, of a great gulf fixed between the successive personalities of a single individuality and all others. It is this instinct which lends its horror of quiet darkness to death, for death is the dissolution of the individuality and the enfranchisement of the atom of the universal which has been segregated in it. On the other hand it is the instinct of solidarity, however misconstrued or unconfessed, which lends mere consciousness of greatness, otherwise unaccountable, a sense of majesty, utterly, nay ludicrously, beyond that which is warranted by the proportion of his personality to the sum of personalities. It is this which makes a man, however good his will, unable to isolate himself from the general frame of things and to conceive of the universe as going on without him. The universe never did and never will go on without him. It is this which renders it all-essential for his comfort, to feel that he is acting a part of some universal plan or frame of things, thus making some sort of religion or philosophy indispensable to him and rendering the notion of unconnected, isolated action abhorrent to his soul. The opposition in human nature of the two ideas of solidarity and personality may be further illustrated by describing as an expression of the former the sense of the sublime, of the grand, or whatever may be called the instinct of infinity, and on the other hand as an expression of the personality, the desire of being circumscribed, shut in, and bounded, the aversion to vague limitations, the sense of coziness (if I may venture to give a philosophical meaning to that peculiar word) or what may be called the instinct of finity. To the latter class of feelings the former seems to open an abstract, unreal, remote, and frigid cloudland, utterly repugnant to its own warm and cheerful, if confined, precincts.

In turn, the instinct of finity to its opposite seems synonymous with pettiness, with infinitesimality, suggestive of a mean, base, and narrow scope, a low-lying, sensuous atmosphere. Their opposition, whereof the mental experience of every reader will have furnished abundant instances, is another testimony of consciousness to the dual constitution of the human soul.

Much sorrow of man comes from his efforts, in imperfect understanding of his own nature, to crowd his universal life into his personal experience, to grasp and realize with the functions of the finite the suggestions of the infinite. He is thus led to make too much of the joys and sorrows and circumstances of the person. Conscious of universal instincts, his mistake lies in expecting the experiences of the individual to be of like scope. He would have the relationships of the individual endowed with the attributes of the universal. Conscious fully of the individual life, his constant effort is to express, as it were, universal instincts in terms of the individuality. No wonder human joy has such an undertone of sadness, and all the concern of the individual life seems but vanity of vanities. It is the mistake of requiring the finite to meet the criterion of the infinite. The joys and sorrows of the individual are adapted to its scope. To seek in them any complete significance is to tempt disappointment. What man complains of as an incurable incongruity between his soul and its external surroundings and the scope by them imposed, is in the stricter truth an incongruity between the two aspects of his own nature. The remedy is ceasing to confuse them and rendering to each the things of each.

We should ever interpret the finite in us by the infinite, but the infinite by the finite, never. For instance, if we interpret love as a partial realization, under the hindering conditions of individuality, of that complete fusion of souls which is the centripetal tendency of the universal instincts, we sublime our passions so that an experience of the individual life becomes an eloquent revelation of the universal. But, if loving, we dream of such a union, but dream of it as if consistent with self-assertion and the preservation of our personalities, we fall into the absurdity of interpreting the one by the many, the universal by the individual. Personalities cannot absorb each other; their essence is diversity. For our personalities, therefore, we cannot expect a perfect intimacy free from all incompatibility and antagonism, but may only solace ourselves with occasional realization of an ecstasy of ineffable tenderness, transitory glimpses of that oneness of our universal parts which overarches and includes all individual diversities. Looking for a perfect outward harmony and fitting together personalities, even of those best adapted and most passionately attached, we shall ever meet with bitter disappointment, but in the higher plane of this larger life we can always realize that fusion and identity that is the heart of all love.

So, too, in that other great experience of the individual, bereavement by death, if we are able to interpret the many by the one, the individual by the universal, we find great consolation for the death of a friend in reflecting that he has but given up that part of him in which he was diverse and separate from us; that is, his personality is to exist henceforth, as far as we know, wholly in the part in which he is one with us and one with all. Truly, not with our bodily passions can we sympathize with his new life. He no longer bears those traits of personality by which these were roused. Our body and the physical sympathies born of it must needs be bereaved; also those mental traits (equally peculiarities of the individuality) which formerly sympathized with the dead. All these are mortal and miss the mortal parts of the dead. For this bereavement there is no remedy, and it is worthy the tribute of tears. But our real life, the indefeasible consciousness of being, the life of solidarity, which connected with the body so transcended its conditions, we may legitimately believe to survive its decay, nay, perhaps, to be then first set free by that decay, and by this higher life at once in us and in all, we are united to the living and to the dead. For this life of solidarity there is neither past nor present, mortality nor immortality, but life ever present, which dons and doffs the countless and varied guises of individuality as one puts on and takes off his garments.

As individuals, then, we have nothing in common with the dead. In that attitude we cannot commune with them, but as universals we are one with them. Nothing should greatly shake those who have their foundations so deeply fixed. But if we reverse this philosophy and interpret the universal by the individual, then, indeed, our plight is pitiable. We are seeking to super-add the universal to the individual, the infinite to the finite, and for result have an incongruous, unthinkable conception more fruitful in vague questioning and in repining than in belief. Claiming a most undesirable immortality for personal traits that even in this life in the course of a few years so utterly change, we cannot consent to regard as perishable those idiosyncrasies, those mental squints and biases, which by the variation of defects are the only marks of intellectualities. It seems as if without these we should lose our identity. And so indeed we should lose our identity as individuals, so factitious, unsubstantial, easily lost a thing is that, a thing of an earmark more or less.

Who has not often felt in sudden shocks of feeling as if the sense of personal identity, i.e., sense of his connection with his particular individuality, were slipping from him? To such as recall similar experiences, and surely all persons must, they will supply the need of argument in convincing them that the personality is a very precarious possession, held by a thread, which will sustain but a feeble strain. The tendency of the mind to ecstasies, trances, and similar suspensions of the sense of personal identity, at times when the body is in a morbid state, as well as the perfectly healthful exaltations of enthusiasm, are additional illustrations of the same truth. I speak of well-known psychological phenomena, and but parenthetically advert to them in claiming their testimony to the accidental connections of the soul with the personality; the latter being, as it were, attached for fair-weather purposes only, by joints that show their seams in every strain of the machine.

To return to the argument: in losing our personal identity, we should become conscious of our other, our universal identity, the identity of a universal solidarity—not losable in the universe, for it fills it. Let us then play with our individual lives as with toys, building them into beautiful forms and delighting ourselves in so brave a game; for have we not our true life, our impregnable citadel of being, as safe from the mishaps of the individual as the serene stars are safe from the earth's uproar and confusion? Be not careful, then, of your goings and doings. Be not deluded into magnifying their importance. Live with a certain calm abandon, a serene and generous recklessness. The things of the individual are at best but trifles, the rents of tinsel in the garment of a day. Be not hard or mean in spending your lives. Be not miserly in hoarding them. What parsimony could seem so supremely laughable in the eyes of onlooking God? It is like the demented millionaire who saves his crusts. The individuality is of so little importance, of such trifling scope, that it should matter little to us what renunciations of its things we make, what inequalities, what deprivations in its experiences we endure. We should hold our lives loosely, and not with the convulsive grip of one who counts personal life his all. The workman does not sacrifice himself to his tools; so should we not seek to serve the individual, which is the serf of the universal, by any sacrifice of those universal instincts, whereof the chief is unselfishness, which constitute true morality.

Our lives are comedy. In the universal there is no tragedy, and in the realm of the individual the experiences are too trifling for the dignity of tragedy. Melancholy and grief, fate or accident, never triumph over the true life of man, only over that transient and unimportant phase of it known as the personality. Justly regarded, human life is a delightful game of passions and calculating, superior in interest to chess on account of the sense of partial identity with the personalities which serve us as puppets, while at the same time that sense of identity, at least to a philosopher's mind, is so incomplete as to prevent the interest from attaining a painful degree of intensity.

Seeing there is in every human being a soul common in nature with all other souls, but in a measure isolated by the conditions of individuality, it is easy to understand the origin of that cardinal motive of human life which is a tendency and a striving to absorb or be absorbed in or united with other lives and all life. This passion for losing ourselves in others or for absorbing them into ourselves, which rebels against individuality as an impediment, is then the expression of the greatest law of solidarity. So long as the particle of this life of solidarity within us is hindered by individual conditions from merging with the rest, that is with the all, so long will desire and the pathos of its partial disappointment be an underlying fact of human nature. It is the operation of this law in great and low things, in the love of men for women, and for each other, for the race, for nature, and for those great ideas which are the symbols of solidarity, that has ever made up the web and woof of human passion. Love between individuals is the attraction between kindred particles, but the greatest of all loves, at once the most enthusiastic, the most sustaining, the most insatiable love of loves is that of an

individual for his remnant, the universe. This is the love of
God by whatever name men may choose to call it. The manner
in which love asserts itself between individuals is illustrative
of its genesis in the law of solidarity. It is the nature of our
souls to fuse together, for they are one, but by the conditions
of individuality, the particle in each one of us is, as it were,
fenced about and shut into itself. There it pines in loneliness,
breeding infinite discontent and prompting all manner of
godlike movings, which mightily disquiet the individual as
to what may be the nature of this inmate which spurns in such
lordly fashion surroundings which fit the individual so well.
It holds to reason that the restless soul will take advantage of
any relaxation in the rigor of the conditions of the individuality to flow out toward its fellow particles and essay fusion
with them. This relaxation may result either from a correlation of the physical or mental faculties of individuals, or it
may result from habitual association and the mutual accom-
modation of faculties resulting therefrom. The sexual relation
is the greatest example of that physical correlation which,
approximating the individualities and relaxing the rigor of
their natural attitude of mutual antagonism and exclusiveness, affords an opportunity for the confluence in at least a
partial sympathy of the roles of lovers, and the bliss resulting
from the consciousness of even this imperfect union is a proof
of the common essence of souls. But after all, how imperfect is
this union, even when helped to the utmost by physical conditions. You find a woman at whose face . . . [you] never tire of
gazing, with a desire miraculously filling a full heart fuller.
Fortune gives her to your arms, and the fruit of physical
satiety has been yours. But is your desire satisfied? Can it thus
be other than mocked? It is herself, her soul, her utter life
which you would absorb, into which you would be absorbed,
and with which you would be one. There is a lust of soul for
soul dwarfing the lust of body for body, as the universal
dwarfs the individual; a lust insatiable, a passion hopeless yet
entrancing, sweeter in desire than all others in consummation.
The poet lover finds not much difference whether the bodily

embraces of his mistress be granted or denied him. He knows that nothing could satisfy his passion, and counts the physical possession a thing almost indifferent to the attainment of his dreams.

Thus much of the hunger of souls for each other is born of the physical correlation of the individualities. But such a sympathy may spring as well from a mental correlation which is only of the individual. Such an adaptation of mind to mind that their natural antagonisms are relaxed produces this form of partial realization of soul solidarity. Intellectual companionships are of this nature. But there is another kind of soul sympathy and tendency to oneness. I refer to that which springs from family life, that which endears with an altogether peculiar and intimate endearment brothers and sisters, the members of one household from childhood; this, too, without any apparent original correlation, mental or physical, between the persons. Nevertheless the correlation exists, only here it is the result of the attrition of habitual intercourse. As the roughest surfaces, by dint of constantly rubbing against each other, become at last smooth or adapt their qualities to each other's forms, so persons associated in the close and constant relationships of family life become at last so fitted to each other that their souls naturally flow together. This is the genesis of family love. Nay, it is this super-induced correlation of habit that lends an element, frequently the largest element, to post-nuptial love. It is the gentle work of time that mends the blunders of the blind god, and binds closely individuals with but small original physical or mental correlation.

Besides the physical correlation between the sexes, there is also a sex of intellect, thus affording a twofold correlation, a cord not easily broken. And when the mutual confluence of souls thus induced has been perfected by the added influence of long habits of intimacy, we have an example of the most complete realization of soul fusion that intercourse permits. It is not to be supposed, then, that the difficulty we find in sympathizing with some persons arises from lack of soul in them, but rather from lack of mental or physical correlation between us. Paradoxical as it may seem, the most perfect lover

given us on earth is our own lover, not because of special
adaptation of his soul to ours, for the essence of all souls is
one, but by reason of our special mutual mental and physical
adaptation, which, relaxing the mutual antagonisms of our
personalities, allows the spirits to fuse. Individualities may or
may not match well. Here is room for choice, but souls always
match, for they are inhalations of one breath, tongues of one
flame.

It seems that at some times the sympathy of solidarity asserts
itself in connection with states of physical exaltation, and
sometimes quite independently of them. Thus, narcotics, in-
toxicants, and the natural stimulants of beauty, music, a soft
bland air, perfume, often produce singly or unitedly a state
very favorable to this psychical experience. They are thus
influential, I suppose, by virtue of relaxing the rigor of individual conditions, as it were, laying the petty, petulant instincts of the personality under a spell. This must be the manner of their operation, for it seems that the languor of the
faculties resulting from extreme exhaustion is equally favorable to the same psychical experience. I conclude, then, that
the physical condition favorable to it is that of suspension of
the sense of wants and requirements of the body, which end is
attained either from their satisfaction or their torpor from
narcotics or from exhaustion. But, as above intimated, the
instincts of universal solidarity also assert themselves quite
independently of physical conditions, responding to direct
moral appeal, to eloquence of speech or written word, or to
the description of beauty or sublimity.

The union of the physical influences described, with those
of a more purely moral nature, produces more remarkable
effects than either class alone; as, when the inspiration of
martial music, combining with the instinct of nationalism
(which is one of the soldierly forms of solidarity), the heart of
the soldier melts in a happy rapture of self-devotion. He is
impatient to throw his life away and rejoices in his body as a
sacrifice which he can make for his country, even as the priest
rejoices in a victim for the altar of his god.

It is this mixture of the physical and moral influences that gives its wonderful power to music combined with religious service. Room fails me for the crowding illustrations of this point. The beauties, sublimities, and infinities of nature are, however, the most constant reminders to the instinct of solidarity. The sky and the sea are two types of infinity that should always suffice to recall us from absorption in the individual side of our nature. They are the material symbols of the soul's infinity, and as the piety of the Romanist revives at the sight of the crucifix, so should the religion of universal solidarity stir freshly in us whenever our eyes are raised to the bottomless vault of heaven or scan the unbounded sea.

In the religion of solidarity is found the only rational philosophy of the moral instincts. Unselfishness, self-sacrifice, are the essence of morality. On the theory of ultimate individualities, unselfishness is madness; but on the theory of the dual life, of which the life of solidarity is abiding and that of the individual transitory, unselfishness is but the sacrifice of the lesser self to the greater self, an eminently rational and philosophical proceeding *per se,* and entirely regardless of ulterior considerations. The moral intuitions which impel to self-sacrifice are the instincts of the life of solidarity asserting themselves against the instincts of the individuality. Hence the majesty beyond appeal in their monitions. As the individuality has its appetites and passions, so the universal life has its passions of self-debasement, its rebellious, self-torturing sympathies, its generous longings. The individuality would always sacrifice other individualities to itself, but the soul of solidarity within us is equally indifferent to all individualities; having in view only the harmony of the universal life as its exigencies require, impels now the sacrifice of my individuality, now of yours. Perhaps it may well be said here that unselfishness according to the religion of solidarity is as inconsistent with undue self-abnegation as with undue self-assertion. It requires in all cases the fulfillment of the instinct of the whole, which may indifferently coincide with the assertion or abnegation of any particular individuality. A bias in favor of altruism is as obnoxious to its principles as the contrary bias in favor of self.

If the thought occur that the soul of solidarity so removed from all affectations of individuality can scarcely be supposed to inspire principles of individual conduct, it suffices to remember that the soul of solidarity is primarily an instinct of an identity of oneness. In the inorganic world we may imagine it as the attraction of cohesion. In the various orders of animated nature it appears in the shape of varied laws of mutual independence and attractions. Manifested in men it takes the form of loyalty or patriotism, philanthropy or sympathy. According to the different forms of individualizations which it animates, the soul of solidarity variously but invariably exerts its centripetal tendency, but its law is always to bind the members of each order first to their own system, and then to the sum of all systems, even as in celestial mechanics the force of gravitation first and most evidently binds the single systems together, and then sends all systems alike revolving about some great single center. Thus it is that men are conscious first of the solidarity of the race; then more dimly of that of the universe.

The secret of many diversities in human character consists in the comparative development of the universal and individual life. Poets, mystics, dreamers, seers, and all of that ilk are marked by an overpowering sense of their element of universal soul. On the other hand, men of affairs, energetic, self-asserting, pushing people have in general their universal instincts imperfectly developed. Given great powers, of such men are made Napoleons and Caesars. Yet such as these are great on the individual plane only. He who has but glimmering visions of the universal stands on a plane infinitely above them. They are great as individuals, a sort of pygmy greatness not to be desired.

All human knowledge consists in the apprehension of differences and resemblances, discords and harmonies of the universe, in analysis and synthesis, in distinction and generalization. The former or analyzing faculties pertain peculiarly to natures strongly developed on the individual side. The latter, the synthetical faculty, the disposition to perceive harmonies and unities rather than discords and differences, is characteristic of natures more open on the side toward the universe, in which the instincts of general solidarity are more vivid. What we call talent exists with characters in which the individual side is predominant; but genius, which is but a vivid realization of the universal, is the dower only of natures dominated by impulses from that side. The genius is never self-conscious while the afflatus is upon him. He is beside himself and thus delivers his oracle of the universal, himself a priest of the infinite.

Telescopic and microscopic are the two windows through which man looks out, the former opening on the infinite, the latter on the infinitesimal. Neither window should be obscured or ignored. Not the Indian Buddhist in ecstatic contemplation, seeking to merge himself in God in disregard of his active status as an individual; not the self-seeker in the insanity of individualism, concentrating his being in microscopic activities (equally microscopic whether they concern faggots or empires, since they are pursued in the spirit of individualism); neither of these is the ideal man. But rather he whose spirit dwells in the stars and in all time, but whose hands are as deft with the most menial as with the mightiest tasks through which the promptings of the soul of solidarity can find expression, who turns his hands with equal readiness to founding empires and to washing beggars' feet, holding all tasks in equal honor, since with him the infinite motive utterly overshadows the deed itself, at best infinitesimal in all questions of its success or failure. It is indeed a pitiable endeavor that seeks to satisfy the craving for grandeur and boundlessness inherent in the soul by piling Pelion on Ossa in achievements undertaken in the spirit of personal aggrandizement. Alexander, thus seeking to fill the void within him, must needs eternally weep for new worlds to conquer, although forever conquering. Yet there is a possibility, a secret of satisfying even this hunger. But it is not by quantity of deeds, but by quality of motives, the spirit in which the deeds are done. The largest deeds of the individual must forever remain infinitesimal, but the spirit of the meanest deed may be infinite, all-satisfying. Poor Alexander had his problem by the wrong end. As individuals we are indeed limited to a narrow spot in today, but as universalists we inherit all time and space. More and more to make the larger life the true and central, the individual inferior and accidental, be the end of our philosophy.

There is a conscious solidarity of the universe toward the intuition of which we must struggle, that it may become to us not a logical abstraction, but a felt and living fact. As individuals we shall never be complete. The completest man lacks the completion of the rest of the universe. Part, then, with the feeling of the externalibility to the universe, which, coupled with the sense of utter ignorance and powerlessness, is so full of despair. Believe that your sympathy with infinite being, infinite extension, infinite variety, is a pledge of identity. Above all, disabuse your mind of the notion that this life is essentially incomplete and preliminary in its nature and destined to issue in some final state. For this notion there is no warrant in reason nor in proper interpretation of intuitions. Time is not a vestibule of eternity, but a part of it. We are now living our immortal lives. This present life is its own perfect consummation, its own reason and excuse. The life of infinite range that our intuitions promise us lies even now open round about us. The avenues leading to it, the vistas opening upon it, are those universal instincts that continually stir us, and which if followed out would lead us thither. It is our own dull lack of faith that causes us to regard them as of no present but only of future significance, that places our heaven ever in some dim land of tomorrow, instead of all about us in the eternal present.

The individuality dies; the soul never. It is inconceivable how it could taste an immortality more perfect than it now enjoys. Nor can a life of wider scope be imagined than that the soul already takes hold of by its universal instincts, and which by the culture of those instincts is even now, more and infinitely more, realizable by us. But as the Christian believer strives that he may enter into the mystical kingdom of heaven, so also the infinite enlargement of life spoken of awaits only those who strive after it in a like spirit.

In the universal instincts within us we are given sure and

certain lodestones that we must interpret by meditation and follow with enthusiasm and faith, whereof the steadily increasing force and clearness of our intuitions will afford constant justification. Surely a more engaging mode of life than its own infinite enlargement we could not set before us. What respect can be claimed for aspirations after other forms and higher grades of life by those who are too dull to imagine the present infinite potentialities of their souls? When will men learn to interpret their intuitions of heaven and infinite things in the present, instead of forever in the future?

Lest it be supposed that the theory of life set forth in this essay is necessarily atheistical in its conclusions, it may be well to suggest what should be quite obvious, that the method of individualizations, by which a man combines a personal and impersonal being, illustrates a possible mode of existence of superior beings or of a Supreme Being, a being as distinctly personal as is man and . . .

Comments by Edward Bellamy, added to the manuscript in 1887.

I should like this paper to be read to me when I am about to die. This tribute I may render without conceit to the boy of twenty-four who wrote it.

This paper, which was written in 1874, when I was twenty-four, represents the germ of what has been ever since my philosophy of life. This paper, which I never offered for publication, is crude and redundant in style and contains some obvious defects in ratiocinations, lost links which I could now supply, but I have never cared to do so. I could say also much more on the same theme; I could draw from my later experiences, expand it into a volume. This maybe I shall sometime do, should I continue in this state of existence. But I have always been slow to publish my opinion concerning these supreme matters. Yet by this time I begin to feel that this is my ripe judgment of life, and that I should be justified in putting it forth as such.

Last pages seem to be lost, but as I recall the paper, there were but a few more paragraphs, one of them setting forth that the religion of solidarity was in no way inconsistent with belief in a personal God. Since we ourselves are at once personals and individuals, so superior beings might be conceived by the Supreme Being. I believe the argument was so.

[MAN AND GOD] [1]

As we left the station together I said to my companion [Mr. Barton] that if he would excuse the inquiry I should be interested to know what particular sect or religious body he represented.

"My dear Mr. West," was the reply, "your question suggests that my friend Dr. Leete has not probably said much to you about the modern way of regarding religious matters."

"Our conversation has turned but little on that subject," I answered, "but it will not surprise me to learn that your ideas and practices are quite different from those of my day. Indeed, religious ideas and ecclesiastical institutions were already at that time undergoing such rapid and radical decomposition that it was safe to predict if religion were to survive another century it would be under very different forms from any the past had known."

"You have suggested a topic," said my companion, "of the greatest possible interest to me. If you have nothing else to do, and would like to talk a little about it, nothing would give me more pleasure."

Upon receiving the assurance that I had absolutely no occupation except to pick up information about the twentieth century, Mr. Barton said:

"Let us then go into this old church, which you will no doubt have already recognized as a relic of your time. There

[1] [From *Equality*, Chapters XXXI and XXXII.]

we can sit comfortably while we talk, amid surroundings well fitted to our theme."

I then perceived that we stood before one of the last-century church buildings which have been preserved as historical monuments, and, moreover, as it oddly enough fell out, that this particular church was no other than the one my family had always attended, and I as well—that is, whenever I attended any church, which was not often.

"What an extraordinary coincidence!" exclaimed Mr. Barton, when I told him this; "who would have expected it? Naturally, when you revisit a spot so fraught with affecting associations, you will wish to be alone. You must pardon my involuntary indiscretion in proposing to turn in here."

"Really," I replied, "the coincidence is interesting merely, not at all affecting. Young men of my day did not, as a rule, take their church relations very seriously. I shall be interested to see how the old place looks. Let us go in, by all means."

The interior proved to be quite unchanged in essential particulars since the last time I had been within its walls, more than a century before. That last occasion, I well remembered, had been an Easter service, to which I had escorted some pretty country cousins who wanted to hear the music and see the flowers. No doubt the processes of decay had rendered necessary many restorations, but they had been carried out so as to preserve completely the original effects.

Leading the way down the main aisle, I paused in front of the family pew.

"This, Mr. Barton," I said, "is, or was, my pew. It is true that I am a little in arrears on pew rent, but I think I may venture to invite you to sit with me."

I had truly told Mr. Barton that there was very little sentiment connected with such church relations as I had maintained. They were indeed merely a matter of family tradition and social propriety. But in another way I found myself not a little moved, as, dropping into my accustomed place at the head of the pew, I looked about the dim and silent interior. As my eye roved from pew to pew, my imagination called back to life the men and women, the young men and maidens, who had been wont of a Sunday, a hundred years before, to sit in those places. As I recalled their various activities, ambitions, hopes, fears, envies, and intrigues, all dominated, as they had been, by the idea of money possessed, lost, or lusted after, I was impressed not so much with the personal death which had come to these my old acquaintances as by the thought of the completeness with which the whole social scheme in which they had lived and moved and had their being had passed away. Not only were they gone, but their world was gone, and its place knew it no more. How strange, how artificial, how grotesque that world had been!—and yet to them and to me, while I was one of them, it had seemed the only possible mode of existence.

Mr. Barton, with delicate respect for my absorption, waited for me to break the silence.

"No doubt," I said, "since you preserve our churches as curiosities, you must have better ones of your own for use?"

"In point of fact," my companion replied, "we have little or no use for churches at all."

"Ah, yes! I had forgotten for the moment that . . . the telephone [radio], in its present perfection, must indeed have quite dispensed with the necessity of the church as an audience room."

"In other words," replied Mr. Barton, "when we assemble now we need no longer bring our bodies with us. It is a curious paradox that while the telephone and electroscope [television], by abolishing distance as a hindrance to sight and hearing, have brought mankind into a closeness of sympathetic and intellectual rapport never before imagined, they have at the same time enabled individuals, although keeping in closest touch with everything going on in the world, to enjoy, if they choose, a physical privacy, such as one had to be a hermit to command in your day. Our advantages in this respect have so far spoiled us that being in a crowd, which was the matter-of-course penalty you had to pay for seeing or hearing anything interesting, would seem too dear a price to pay for almost any enjoyment."

"I can imagine," I said, "that ecclesiastical institutions

must have been affected in other ways besides the disuse of church buildings, by the general adaptation of the telephone system to religious teaching. In my day, the fact that no speaker could reach by voice more than a small group of hearers made it necessary to have a veritable army of preachers —some fifty thousand, say, in the United States alone—in order to instruct the population. Of these, not one in many hundreds was a person who had anything to utter really worth hearing. For example, we will say that fifty thousand clergymen preached every Sunday as many sermons to as many congregations. Four-fifths of these sermons were poor, half of the rest perhaps fair, some of the others good, and a few score, possibly, out of the whole really of a fine class. Now, nobody, of course, would hear a poor discourse on any subject when he could just as easily hear a fine one, and if we had perfected the telephone system to the point you have, the result would have been, the first Sunday after its introduction, that everybody who wanted to hear a sermon would have connected with the lecture rooms or churches of the few widely celebrated preachers, and the rest would have had no hearers at all, and presently have been obliged to seek new occupations."

Mr. Barton was amused. "You have, in fact, hit," he said, "upon the mechanical side of one of the most important contrasts between your times and ours—namely, the modern suppression of mediocrity in teaching, whether intellectual or religious. Being able to pick from the choicest intellects and most inspired moralists and seers of the generation, everybody of course agrees in regarding it a waste of time to listen to any who have less weighty messages to deliver. When you consider that all are thus able to obtain the best inspiration the greatest minds can give, and couple this with the fact that, thanks to the universality of the higher education, all are at least pretty good judges of what is best, you have the secret of what might be called at once the strongest safeguard of the degree of civilization we have attained, and the surest pledge of the highest possible rate of progress toward ever better conditions—namely, the leadership of moral and intellectual

genius. To one like you, educated according to the ideas of
the nineteenth century as to what democracy meant, it may
seem like a paradox that the equalizing of economic and educational conditions, which has perfected democracy, should
have resulted in the most perfect aristocracy, or government
by the best, that could be conceived; yet what result could
be more matter of course? The people of today, too intelligent
to be misled or abused for selfish ends even by demigods, are
ready, on the other hand, to comprehend and to follow with
enthusiasm every better leading. The result is that our greatest men and women wield today an unselfish empire, more
absolute than your czars dreamed of, and of an extent to
make Alexander's conquests seem provincial. There are men
in the world who, when they choose to appeal to their fellow
men, by the bare announcement are able to command the
simultaneous attention of one to five or eight hundred millions
of people. In fact, if the occasion be a great one, and the
speaker worthy of it, a world-wide silence reigns as in their
various places, some beneath the sun and others under the
stars, some by the light of dawn and others at sunset, all hang
on the lips of the teacher. Such power would have seemed,
perhaps, in your day dangerous, but when you consider that
its tenure is conditional on the wisdom and unselfishness of
its exercise, and would fail with the first false note, you may
judge that it is a dominion as safe as God's."

"Dr. Leete," I said, "has told me something of the way in
which the universality of culture, combined with your
scientific appliances, has made physically possible this leadership of the best; but, I beg your pardon, how could a speaker
address numbers so vast as you speak of unless the pentecostal
miracle were repeated? Surely the audience must be limited
at least by the number of those understanding one language."

"Is it possible that Dr. Leete has not told you of our universal language?"

"I have heard no language but English."

"Of course, everybody talks the language of his own country with his countrymen, but with the rest of the world he

talks the general language—that is to say, we have nowadays to acquire but two languages to talk to all peoples—our own and the universal. We may learn as many more as we please, and we usually please to learn many, but these two are alone needful to go all over the world or to speak across it without an interpreter. A number of the smaller nations have wholly abandoned their national tongue and talk only the general language. The greater nations, which have fine literature embalmed in their languages, have been more reluctant to abandon them, and in this way the smaller folks have actually had a certain sort of advantage over the greater. The tendency, however, to cultivate but one language as a living tongue and to treat all the others as dead or moribund is increasing at such a rate that if you had slept through another generation you might have found none but philological experts able to talk with you."

"But even with the universal telephone and the universal language," I said, "there still remains the ceremonial and ritual side of religion to be considered. For the practice of that I should suppose the piously inclined would still need churches to assemble in, however able to dispense with them for purposes of instruction."

"If any feel that need, there is no reason why they should not have as many churches as they wish and assemble as often as they see fit. I do not know but there are still those who do so. But with a high grade of intelligence become universal the world was bound to outgrow the ceremonial side of religion, which with its forms and symbols, its holy times and places, its sacrifices, feasts, fasts, and new moons, meant so much in the child-time of the race. The time has now fully come which Christ foretold in that talk with the woman by the well of Samaria when the idea of the Temple and all it stood for would give place to the wholly spiritual religion, without respect of times or places, which he declared most pleasing to God."

"With the ritual and ceremonial side of religion outgrown," said I, "with church attendance become superfluous for purposes of instruction, and everybody selecting his own preacher on personal grounds, I should say that sectarian lines must have pretty nearly disappeared."

"Ah, yes!" said Mr. Barton, "that reminds me that our talk began with your inquiry as to what religious sect I belonged to. It is a very long time since it has been customary for people to divide themselves into sects and classify themselves under different names on account of variations of opinion as to matters of religion."

"Is it possible," I exclaimed, "that you mean to say people no longer quarrel over religion? Do you actually tell me that human beings have become capable of entertaining different opinions about the next world without becoming enemies in this? Dr. Leete has compelled me to believe a good many miracles, but this is too much."

"I do not wonder that it seems rather a startling proposition, at first statement, to a man of the nineteenth century," replied Mr. Barton. "But, after all, who was it who started and kept up the quarreling over religion in former days?"

"It was, of course, the ecclesiastical bodies—the priests and preachers."

"But they were not many. How were they able to make so much trouble?"

"On account of the masses of the people who, being densely ignorant, were correspondingly superstitious and bigoted, and were tools in the hands of the ecclesiastics."

"But there was a minority of the cultured. Were they bigoted also? Were they tools of the ecclesiastics?"

"On the contrary, they always held a calm and tolerant attitude on religious questions and were independent of the priesthoods. If they deferred to ecclesiastical influence at all, it was because they held it needful for the purpose of controlling the ignorant populace."

"Very good. You have explained your miracle. There is no ignorant populace now for whose sake it is necessary for the more intelligent to make any compromises with truth. Your cultured class, with their tolerant and philosophical view of religious differences, and the criminal folly of quarreling about them, has become the only class there is."

"How long is it since people ceased to call themselves Catholics, Protestants, Baptists, Methodists, and so on?"

"That kind of classification may be said to have received a fatal shock at the time of the great Revolution, when sectarian demarcations and doctrinal differences, already fallen into a good deal of disregard, were completely swept away and forgotten in the passionate impulse of brotherly love which brought men together for the founding of a nobler social order. The old habit might possibly have revived in time had it not been for the new culture, which, during the first generation subsequent to the Revolution, destroyed the soil of ignorance and superstition which had supported ecclesiastical influence, and made its recrudescence impossible for evermore.

"Although, of course," continued my companion, "the universalizing of intellectual culture is the only cause that needs to be considered in accounting for the total disappearance of religious sectarianism, yet it will give you a more vivid realization of the gulf fixed between the ancient and the modern usages as to religion if you consider certain economic conditions, now wholly passed away, which in your time buttressed the power of ecclesiastical institutions in very substantial ways. Of course, in the first place, church buildings were needful to preach in, and equally so for the ritual and ceremonial side of religion. Moreover, the sanction of religious teaching, depending chiefly on the authority of tradition instead of its own reasonableness, made it necessary for any preacher who would command hearers to enter the service of some of the established sectarian organizations. Religion, in a word, like industry and politics, was capitalized by greater or smaller corporations which exclusively controlled the plant and machinery, and conducted it for the prestige and power of the firms. As all those who desired to engage in politics or industry were obliged to do so in subjection to the individuals and corporations controlling the machinery, so was it in religious matters likewise. Persons desirous of entering on the occupation of religious teaching could do so only by conforming to the conditions of some of the organizations controlling the machinery, plant, and good will of the business —that is to say, of some one of the great ecclesiastical corporations. To teach religion outside of these corporations, when not positively illegal, was a most difficult undertaking, however great the ability of the teacher—as difficult, indeed, as it was to get on in politics without wearing a party badge, or to succeed in business in opposition to the great capitalists. The would-be religious teacher had to attach himself, therefore, to some one or other of the sectarian organizations, whose mouthpiece he must consent to be as the condition of obtaining any hearing at all. The organization might be hierarchical, in which case he took his instructions from above, or it might be congregational, in which case he took his orders from below. The one method was monarchical, the other democratic, but one as inconsistent as the other with the office of the religious teacher, the first condition of which, as we look at it, should be absolute spontaneity of feeling and liberty of utterance.

"It may be said that the old ecclesiastical system depended on a double bondage: first, the intellectual subjection of the masses through ignorance to their spiritual directors; and, secondly, the bondage of the directors themselves to the sectarian organizations, which as spiritual capitalists monopolized the opportunities of teaching. As the bondage was twofold, so also was the enfranchisement—a deliverance alike of the people and of their teachers, who, under the guise of leaders, had been themselves but puppets. Nowadays preaching is as free as hearing and as open to all. The man who feels a special calling to talk to his fellows upon religious themes has no need of any other capital than something worth saying. Given this, without need of any further machinery than the free telephone, he is able to command an audience limited only by the force and fitness of what he has to say. He now does not live by his preaching. His business is not a distinct profession. He does not belong to a

class apart from other citizens, either by education or occupation. It is not needful for any purpose that he should do
so. The higher education which he shares with all others
furnishes ample intellectual equipment, while the abundant
leisure for personal pursuits with which our life is interfused,
and the entire exemption from public duty after forty-five,
give abundant opportunity for the exercise of his vocation. In
a word, the modern religious teacher is a prophet, not a
priest. The sanction of his words lies not in any human
ordination or ecclesiastical *exequatur* [authorization], but,
even as it was with the prophets of old, in such response as
his words may have power to evoke from human hearts."

"If people," I suggested, "still retaining a taste for the
old-time ritual and ceremonial observances and face-to-face
preaching, should desire to have churches and clergy for their
special service, is there anything to prevent it?"

"No, indeed. Liberty is the first and last word of our civilization. It is perfectly consistent with our economic system
for a group of individuals, by contributing out of their in-
comes, not only to rent buildings for group purposes, but
by indemnifying the nation for the loss of an individual's
public service to secure him as their special minister. Though
the state will enforce no private contracts of any sort, it does
not forbid them. The old ecclesiastical system was, for a time
after the Revolution, kept up by remnants in this way, and
might be until now if anybody had wished. But the contempt into which the hireling relation had fallen at once
after the Revolution soon made the position of such hired
clergymen intolerable, and presently there were none who
would demean themselves by entering upon so despised a
relation, and none, indeed, who would have spiritual service, of all others, on such terms."

"As you tell the story," I said, " it seems very plain how
it all came about, and could not have been otherwise; but
you can perhaps hardly imagine how a man of the nineteenth
century, accustomed to the vast place occupied by the
ecclesiastical edifice and influence in human affairs, is affected

by the idea of a world getting on without anything of the sort."

"I can imagine something of your sensation," replied my companion, "though doubtless not adequately. And yet I must say that no change in the social order seems to us to have been more distinctly foreshadowed by the signs of the times in your day than precisely this passing away of the ecclesiastical system. As you yourself observed, just before we came into this church, there was then going on a general deliquescence of dogmatism which made your contemporaries wonder what was going to be left. The influence and authority of the clergy were rapidly disappearing, the sectarian lines were being obliterated, the creeds were falling into contempt, and the authority of tradition was being repudiated. Surely if anything could be safely predicted it was that the religious ideas and institutions of the world were approaching some great change."

"Doubtless," said I, "if the ecclesiastics of my day had regarded the result as merely depending on the drift of opinion among men, they would have been inclined to give up all hope of retaining their influence, but there was another element in the case which gave them courage."

"And what was that?"

"The women. They were in my day called the religious sex. The clergy generally were ready to admit that so far as the interest of the cultured class of men, and indeed of the men generally, in the churches went, they were in a bad way, but they had faith that the devotion of the women would save the cause. Woman was the sheet anchor of the church. Not only were women the chief attendants at religious functions, but it was largely through their influence on the men that the latter tolerated, even so far as they did, the ecclesiastical pretensions. Now, were not our clergymen justified in counting on the continued support of women, whatever the men might do?"

"Certainly they would have been if woman's position was to remain unchanged, but, as you are doubtless by this time well aware, the elevation and enlargement of woman's sphere in all directions was perhaps the most notable single aspect of the Revolution. When women were called the religious sex it would have been indeed a high ascription if it had been meant that they were the more spiritually-minded, but that was not at all what the phrase signified to those who used it; it was merely intended to put in a complimentary way the fact that women in your day were the docile sex. Less educated, as a rule, than men, unaccustomed to responsibility, and trained in habits of subordination and self-distrust, they leaned in all things upon precedent and authority. Naturally, therefore, they still held to the principle of authoritative teaching in religion long after men had generally rejected it. All that was changed with the Revolution, and indeed began to change long before it. Since the Revolution there has been no difference in the education of the sexes nor in the independence of their economic and social position in the exercise of responsibility or experience in the practical conduct of affairs. As you might naturally infer, they are no longer, as formerly, a peculiarly docile class, nor have they any more toleration for authority, whether in religion, politics, or economics, than their brethren. In every pursuit of life they join with men on equal terms, including the most important and engrossing of all our pursuits—the search after knowledge concerning the nature and destiny of man and his relation to the spiritual and material infinity of which he is a part."

"I [2] infer, then," I said, "that the disappearance of religious divisions and the priestly caste has not operated to lessen the general interest in religion."

"Should you have supposed that it would so operate?"

"I don't know. I never gave much thought to such matters. The ecclesiastical class represented that they were very essential to the conservation of religion, and the rest of us took it for granted that it was so."

"Every social institution which has existed for a consid-

[2] [From Chapter XXXII.]

erable time," replied Mr. Barton, "has doubtless performed
some function which was at the time more or less useful
and necessary. Kings, ecclesiastics, and capitalists—all of
them, for that matter, merely different sorts of capitalists—
have, no doubt, in their proper periods, performed functions
which, however badly discharged, were necessary and could
not then have been discharged in any better manner. But just
as the abolition of royalty was the beginning of decent
government, just as the abolition of private capitalism was
the beginning of effective wealth production, so the disappearance of church organization and machinery, or ecclesiastical capitalism, was the beginning of a world-awakening
of impassioned interest in the vast concerns covered by the
word religion.

"Necessary as may have been the subjection of the race to
priestly authority in the course of human evolution, it was
the form of tutelage which, of all others, was most calculated to benumb and deaden the faculties affected by it, and
the collapse of ecclesiasticism presently prepared the way
for an enthusiasm of interest in the great problems of human
nature and destiny which would have been scarcely conceivable by the worthy ecclesiastics of your day who with
such painful efforts and small results sought to awake their
flocks to spiritual concerns. The lack of general interest in
these questions in your time was the natural result of their
monopoly as the special province of the priestly class whose
members stood as interpreters between man and the mystery
about him, undertaking to guarantee the spiritual welfare
of all who would trust them. The decay of priestly authority
left every soul face to face with that mystery, with the responsibility of its interpretation upon himself. The collapse
of the traditional theologies relieved the whole subject of
man's relation with the infinite from the oppressive effect
of the false finalities of dogma which had till then made the
most boundless of sciences the most cramped and narrow.
Instead of the mind-paralyzing worship of the past and the
bondage of the present to that which is written, the conviction took hold on men that there was no limit to what

they might know concerning their nature and destiny, and no limit to that destiny. The priestly idea that the past was diviner than the present, that God was behind the race, gave place to the belief that we should look forward and not backward for inspiration, and that the present and the future promised a fuller and more certain knowledge concerning the soul and God than any the past had attained."

"Has this belief," I asked, "been thus far practically confirmed by any progress actually made in the assurance of what is true as to these things? Do you consider that you really know more about them than we did, or that you know more positively the things which we merely tried to believe?"

Mr. Barton paused a moment before replying.

"You remarked a little while ago," he said, "that your talks with Dr. Leete had as yet turned little on religious matters. In introducing you to the modern world it was entirely right and logical that he should dwell at first mainly upon the change in economic systems, for that has, of course, furnished the necessary material basis for all the other changes that have taken place. But I am sure that you will never meet anyone who, being asked in what direction the progress of the race during the past century has tended most to increase human happiness, would not reply that it had been in the science of the soul and its relation to the Eternal and Infinite.

"This progress has been the result not merely of a more rational conception of the subject, and complete intellectual freedom in its study, but largely also of social conditions which have set us almost wholly free from material engrossments. We have now for nearly a century enjoyed an economic welfare which has left nothing to be wished for in the way of physical satisfactions, especially as in proportion to the increase of this abundance there has been through culture a development of simplicity in taste which rejects excess and surfeit and ever makes less and less of the material side of life and more of the mental and moral. Thanks to this cooperation of the material with the moral evolution, the more we have the less we need. Long ago it came to be recognized that on the material side the race had reached the goal of its evolution. We have practically lost ambition for further progress in that direction. The natural result has been that for a long period the main energies of the intellect have been concentrated upon the possibilities of the spiritual evolution of mankind for which the completion of its material evolution has but prepared the beginning. What we have so far learned we are convinced is but the first faint inkling of the knowledge we shall attain to; and yet if the limitations of this earthly state were such that we might never hope here to know more than now, we should not repine, for the knowledge we have has sufficed to turn the shadow of death into a bow of promise and distill the saltness out of human tears. You will observe, as you shall come to know more of our literature, that one respect in which it differs from yours is the total lack of the tragic note. This has very naturally followed from a conception of our real life as having an inaccessible security, 'hid in God,' as Paul said, whereby the accidents and vicissitudes of the personality are reduced to relative triviality.

"Your seers and poets in exalted moments had seen that death was but a step in life, but this seemed to most of you to have been a hard saying. Nowadays, as life advances toward its close, instead of being shadowed by gloom it is marked by an access of impassioned expectancy which would cause the young to envy the old, but for the knowledge that in a little while the same door will be opened to them. In your day the undertone of life seems to have been one of unutterable sadness, which, like the moaning of the sea to those who live near the ocean, made itself audible whenever for a moment the noise and bustle of petty engrossments ceased. Now this undertone is so exultant that we are still to hear it."

"If men go on," I said, "growing at this rate in the knowledge of divine things and the sharing of the divine life, what will they yet come to?"

Mr. Barton smiled.

"Said not the serpent in the old story, 'If you eat of the fruit of the tree of knowledge you shall be as gods'? The promise was true in words, but apparently there was some mistake about the tree. Perhaps it was the tree of selfish knowledge, or else the fruit was not ripe. The story is obscure. Christ later said the same thing when he told men that they might be the sons of God. But he made no mistake as to the tree he showed them, and the fruit was ripe. It was the fruit of love, for universal love is at once the seed and fruit, cause and effect, of the highest and completest knowledge. Through boundless love man becomes a god, for thereby is he made conscious of his oneness with God, and all things are put under his feet. It has been only since the great Revolution brought in the era of human brotherhood that mankind has been able to eat abundantly of this fruit of the true tree of knowledge, and thereby grow more and more into the consciousness of the divine soul as the essential self and the true hiding of our lives. Yes, indeed, we shall be gods. The motto of the modern civilization is 'Eritis sicut Deus' " [Ye shall be as gods].

"You speak of Christ. Do I understand that this modern religion is considered by you to be the same doctrine Christ taught?"

"Most certainly. It has been taught from the beginning of history and doubtless earlier, but Christ's teaching is that which has most fully and clearly come down to us. It was the doctrine that he taught, but the world could not then receive it save a few, nor indeed has it ever been possible for the world in general to receive it or even to understand it until this present century."

"Why could not the world receive earlier the revelation it seems to find so easy of comprehension now?"

"Because," replied Mr. Barton, "the prophet and revealer of the soul and of God, which are the same, is love, and until these latter days the world refused to hear love, but crucified him. The religion of Christ, depending as it did upon the

experience and intuitions of the unselfish enthusiasms, could
not possibly be accepted or understood generally by a world
which tolerated a social system based upon fratricidal struggle
as the condition of existence. Prophets, messiahs, seers, and
saints might indeed for themselves see God face to face, but
it was impossible that there should be any general apprehension of God as Christ saw Him until social justice had
brought in brotherly love. Man must be revealed to man as
brother before God could be revealed to him as father.
Nominally, the clergy professed to accept and repeat Christ's
teaching that God is a loving father, but of course it was
simply impossible that any such idea should actually germ-
inate and take root in hearts as cold and hard as stone
toward their fellow beings and sodden with hate and suspicion
of them. 'If a man love not his brother whom he hath seen,
how shall he love God whom he hath not seen?' The priests
deafened their flocks with appeals to love God, to give their
hearts to Him. They should have rather taught them, as
Christ did, to love their fellow men and give their hearts to
them. Hearts so given the love of God would presently en-
kindle, even as, according to the ancients, fire from heaven
might be depended on to ignite a sacrifice fitly prepared
and laid.

"From the pulpit yonder, Mr. West, doubtless you have
many times heard these words and many like them repeated:
'If we love one another, God dwelleth in us and His love is
perfected in us.' 'He that loveth his brother dwelleth in the
light.' 'If any man say I love God, and hateth his brother, he
is a liar.' 'He that loveth not his brother, abideth in death.'
'God is love, and he that dwelleth in love dwelleth in God.'
'Everyone that loveth, knoweth God.' 'He that loveth not,
knoweth not God.'

"Here is the very distillation of Christ's teaching as to
the conditions of entering on the divine life. In this we find
sufficient explanation why the revelation which came to
Christ so long ago and to other illumined souls could not
possibly be received by mankind in general so long as an

inhuman social order made a wall between man and God, and why, the moment that wall was cast down, the revelation flooded the earth like a sunburst.

" 'If we love one another, God dwelleth in us,' and mark how the words were made good in the way by which at last the race found God! It was not, remember, by directly, purposely, or consciously seeking God. The great enthusiasm of humanity which overthrew the old order and brought in the fraternal society was not primarily or consciously a godward aspiration at all. It was essentially a humane movement. It was a melting and flowing forth of men's hearts toward one another, a rush of contrite, repentant tenderness, an impassioned impulse of mutual love and self-devotion to the commonweal. But 'if we love one another, God dwelleth in us,' and so men found it. It appears that there came a moment, the most transcendent moment in the history of the race of man, when with the fraternal glow of this world of new-found embracing brothers there seems to have mingled the ineffable thrill of a divine participation, as if the hand of God were clasped over the joined hands of men. And so it has continued to this day and shall forevermore."

[MR. BARTON'S SERMON] [1]

. . . Dr. Leete asked me if I would care to hear a sermon. . . . "I see by the paper [he said] that Mr. Barton is to preach this morning, and he preaches only by telephone, and to audiences often reaching 150,000."

"The novelty of the experience of hearing a sermon under such circumstances would incline me to be one of Mr. Barton's hearers, if for no other reason," I said.

An hour or two later, as I sat reading in the library, Edith came for me, and I followed her to the music room, where

---

[1] [From *Looking Backward*, Chapter XXVI.]

Dr. and Mrs. Leete were waiting. We had not more than seated ourselves comfortably when the tinkle of a bell was heard, and a few moments after . . . [a familiar] voice . . . at the pitch of ordinary conversation, addressed us, with an effect of proceeding from an invisible person in the room. This was what the voice said:

"We have had among us, during the past week, a critic from the nineteenth century, a living representative of the epoch of our great-grandparents. It would be strange if a fact so extraordinary had not somewhat strongly affected our imaginations. Perhaps most of us have been stimulated to some effort to realize the society of a century ago, and figure to ourselves what it must have been like to live then. In inviting you now to consider certain reflections upon this subject which have occurred to me, I presume that I shall rather follow than divert the course of your own thoughts."

Edith whispered something to her father at this point, to which he nodded assent and turned to me.

"Mr. West," he said, "Edith suggests that you may find it slightly embarrassing to listen to a discourse on the lines Mr. Barton is laying down, and if so, you need not be cheated out of a sermon. She will connect us with Mr. Sweetser's speaking room if you say so, and I can still promise you a very good discourse."

"No, no," I said. "Believe me, I would much rather hear what Mr. Barton has to say."

"As you please," replied my host.

When her father spoke to me Edith had touched a screw, and the voice of Mr. Barton had ceased abruptly. Now at another touch the room was once more filled with the earnest sympathetic tones which had already impressed me most favorably.

"I venture to assume that one effect has been common with us as a result of this effort at retrospection, and that it has been to leave us more than ever amazed at the stupendous change which one brief century has made in the material and moral conditions of humanity.

"Still, as regards the contrast between the poverty of the nation and the world in the nineteenth century and their wealth now, it is not greater, possibly, than had been before seen in human history, perhaps not greater, for example, than that between the poverty of this country during the earliest colonial period of the seventeenth century and the relatively great wealth it had attained at the close of the nineteenth, or between the England of William the Conqueror and that of Victoria. Although the aggregate riches of a nation did not then, as now, afford any accurate criterion of the [condition of] masses of its people, yet instances like these afford partial parallels for the merely material side of the contrast between the nineteenth and the twentieth centuries. It is when we contemplate the moral aspect of that contrast that we find ourselves in the presence of a phenomenon for which history offers no precedent, however far back we may cast our eye. One might almost be excused who should exclaim, 'Here, surely, is something like a miracle!' Nevertheless, when we give over idle wonder and begin to examine the seeming prodigy critically, we find it no prodigy at all, much less a miracle. It is not necessary to suppose a moral new birth of humanity, or a wholesale destruction of the wicked and survival of the good, to account for the fact before us. It finds its simple and obvious explanation in the reaction of a changed environment upon human nature. It means merely that a form of society which was founded on the pseudo self-interest of selfishness, and appealed solely to the anti-social and brutal side of human nature, has been replaced by institutions based on the true self-interest of a rational unselfishness, and appealing to the social and generous instincts of men.

"My friends, if you would see men again the beasts of prey they seemed in the nineteenth century, all you have to do is to restore the old social and industrial system, which taught them to view their natural prey in their fellow men, and find their gain in the loss of others. No doubt it seems to you that no necessity, however dire, would have tempted you to subsist on what superior skill or strength enabled you to wrest from others equally needy. But suppose it were not merely your own life that you were responsible for. I know well that there must have been many a man among our ancestors who, if it had been merely a question of his own life, would sooner have given it up than nourished it by bread snatched from others. But this he was not permitted to do. He had dear lives dependent on him. Men loved women in those days, as now. God knows how they dared be fathers, but they had babies as sweet, no doubt, to them as ours to us, whom they must feed, clothe, educate. The gentlest creatures are fierce when they have young to provide for, and in that wolfish society the struggle for bread borrowed a peculiar desperation from the tenderest sentiments. For the sake of those dependent on him, a man might not choose, but must plunge into the foul fight—cheat, overreach, supplant, defraud, buy below worth and sell above, break down the business by which his neighbor fed his young ones, tempt men to buy what they ought not and to sell what they should not, grind his laborers, sweat his debtors, cozen his creditors. Though a man sought it carefully with tears, it was hard to find a way in which he could earn a living and provide for his family except by pressing in before some weaker rival and taking the food from his mouth. Even the ministers of religion were not exempt from this cruel necessity. While they warned their flocks against the love of money, regard for their families compelled them to keep an outlook for the pecuniary prizes of their calling. Poor fellows, theirs was indeed a trying business, preaching to men a generosity and unselfishness which they and everybody knew would, in the existing state of the world, reduce to poverty those who should practice them, laying down laws of conduct which the law of self-preservation compelled men to break. Looking on the inhuman spectacle of society, these worthy men bitterly bemoaned the depravity of human nature; as if angelic nature would not have been debauched in such a devil's school! Ah, my friends, believe me, it is not now in this happy age that humanity is proving the divinity within it. It was rather in those evil days when not even the fight for life with one another, the struggle for mere existence, in which mercy was folly, could wholly banish generosity and kindness from the earth.

"It is not hard to understand the desperation with which men and women, who under other conditions would have been full of gentleness and truth, fought and tore each other in the scramble for gold, when we realize what it meant to miss it, what poverty was in that day. For the body it was hunger and thirst, torment by heat and frost, in sickness neglect, in health unremitting toil; for the moral nature it meant oppression, contempt, and the patient endurance of indignity, brutish associations from infancy, the loss of all the innocence of childhood, the grace of womanhood, the dignity of manhood; for the mind it meant the death of ignorance, the torpor of all those faculties which distinguish us from brutes, the reduction of life to a round of bodily functions.

"Ah, my friends, if such a fate as this were offered you and your children as the only alternative of success in the accumulation of wealth, how long do you fancy would you be in sinking to the moral level of your ancestors?

"Some two or three centuries ago an act of barbarity was committed in India, which, though the number of lives destroyed was but a few score, was attended by such peculiar horrors that its memory is likely to be perpetual. A number of English prisoners were shut up in a room containing not enough air to supply one-tenth their number. The unfortunates were gallant men, devoted comrades in service, but, as the agonies of suffocation began to take hold on them, they forgot all else and became involved in a hideous struggle, each one for himself and against all others, to force a way to one of the small apertures of the prison at which alone it was possible to get a breath of air. It was a struggle in which men became beasts, and the recital of its horrors by the few survivors so shocked our forefathers that for a century later we find it a stock reference in their literature as a typical illustration of the extreme possibilities of human misery, as shocking in its moral as its physical aspect. They could scarcely have anticipated that to us that Black Hole of Calcutta, with its press of maddened men tearing and trampling one another in the struggle to win a place at the breathing holes, would seem a striking type of the society of their age. It lacked something of being a complete type, however, for in the Calcutta Black Hole there were no tender women, no little children and old men and women, no cripples. They were at least all men, strong to bear, who suffered.

"When we reflect that the ancient order of which I have been speaking was prevalent up to the end of the nineteenth century, while to us the new order which succeeded it already seems antique, even our parents having known no other, we cannot fail to be astounded at the suddenness with which a transition so profound, beyond all previous experience of the race, must have been effected. Some observation of the state of men's minds during the last quarter of the nineteenth century will, however, in great measure, dissipate this astonishment. Though general intelligence in the modern sense could not be said to exist in any community at that time, yet, as compared with previous generations, the one then on the stage was intelligent. The inevitable consequence of even this comparative degree of intelligence had been a perception of the evils of society, such as had never before been general. It is quite true that these evils had been even worse, much worse, in previous ages. It was the increased intelligence of the masses which made the difference, as the dawn reveals the squalor of surroundings which in the darkness may have seemed tolerable. The keynote of the literature of the period was one of compassion for the poor and unfortunate, and indignant outcry against the failure of the social machinery to ameliorate the miseries of men. It is plain from these outbursts that the moral hideousness of the spectacle about them was, at least by flashes, fully realized by the best of the men of that time, and that the lives of some of the more sensitive and generous-hearted of them were rendered well-nigh unendurable by the intensity of their sympathies.

"Although the idea of the vital unity of the family of mankind, the reality of human brotherhood, was very far from being apprehended by them as the moral axiom it seems to us, yet it is a mistake to suppose that there was no feeling at all corresponding to it. I could read you passages of great beauty from some of their writers which show that the conception was clearly attained by a few, and no doubt vaguely by many more. Moreover, it must not be forgotten that the nineteenth century was in name Christian, and the fact that the entire commercial and industrial frame of society was the embodiment of the anti-Christian spirit must have had some weight, though I admit it was strangely little, with the nominal followers of Jesus Christ.

"When we inquire why it did not have more, why, in general, long after a vast majority of men had agreed as to the crying abuses of the existing social arrangement, they still tolerated it or contented themselves with talking of petty reforms in it, we come upon an extraordinary fact. It was the sincere belief of even the best of men at that epoch that the only stable elements in human nature, on which a social system could be safely founded, were its worst propensities. They had been taught and believed that greed and self-seeking were all that held mankind together, and that all human associations would fall to pieces if anything were done to blunt the edge of these motives or curb their operation. In a word, they believed—even those who longed to believe otherwise—the exact reverse of what seems to us self-evident; they believed, that is, that the anti-social qualities of men, and not their social qualities, were what furnished the cohesive force of society. It seemed reasonable to them that men lived together solely for the purpose of overreaching and oppressing one another, and of being overreached and oppressed, and that while a society that gave full scope to these propensities could stand, there would be little chance for one based on the idea of co-operation for the benefit of all. It seems absurd to expect anyone to believe that convictions like these were ever seriously entertained by men; but that they were not only entertained by our great-grandfathers, but were responsible for the long delay in doing away with the ancient order, after a conviction of its intolerable abuses had become general, is as well established as any fact in history can be. Just here you will find the explanation of the profound pessimism of the literature of the last quarter of the nineteenth century, the note of melancholy in its poetry, and the cynicism of its humor.

"Feeling that the condition of the race was unendurable, they had no clear hope of anything better. They believed that the evolution of humanity had resulted in leading it into a *cul de sac,* and that there was no way of getting forward. The frame of men's minds at this time is strikingly illustrated by treatises which have come down to us, and may even now be consulted in our libraries by the curious, in which laborious arguments are pursued to prove that despite the evil plight of men, life was still, by some slight preponderance of considerations, probably better worth living than leaving. Despising themselves, they despised their Creator. There was a general decay of religious belief. Pale and watery gleams, from skies thickly veiled by doubt and dread, alone lighted up the chaos of earth. That men should doubt Him whose breath is in their nostrils, or dread the hands that molded them, seems to us indeed a pitiable insanity; but we must remember that children who are brave by day have sometimes foolish fears at night. The dawn has come since then. It is very easy to believe in the fatherhood of God in the twentieth century.

"Briefly, as must needs be in a discourse of this character, I have adverted to some of the causes which had prepared men's minds for the change from the old to the new order, as well as some causes of the conservatism of despair which for a while held it back after the time was ripe. To wonder at the rapidity with which the change was completed after its possibility was first entertained is to forget the intoxicating effect of hope upon minds long accustomed to despair. The sunburst, after so long and dark a night, must needs have had a dazzling effect. From the moment men allowed them- selves to believe that humanity after all had not been meant for a dwarf, that its squat stature was not the measure of its possible growth, but that it stood upon the verge of an avatar of limitless development, the reaction must needs have been overwhelming. It is evident that nothing was able to stand against the enthusiasm which the new faith inspired.

"Here, at last, men must have felt, was a cause compared with which the grandest of historic causes have been trivial. It was doubtless because it could have commanded millions of martyrs, that none were needed. The change of a dynasty in a petty kingdom of the old world often cost more lives than did the Revolution which set the feet of the human race at last in the right way.

"Doubtless it ill beseems one to whom the boon of life in our resplendent age has been vouchsafed to wish his destiny other, and yet I have often thought that I would fain exchange my share in this serene and golden day for a place in that stormy epoch of transition, when heroes burst the barred gate of the future and revealed to the kindling gaze of a hopeless race, in place of the blank wall that had closed its path, a vista of progress whose end, for very excess of light, still dazzles us. Ah, my friends! who will say that to have lived then, when the weakest influence was a lever to whose touch the centuries trembled, was not worth a share even in this era of fruition?

"You know the story of that last, greatest, and most blood- less of revolutions. In the time of one generation men laid aside the social traditions and practices of barbarians, and assumed a social order worthy of rational and human beings. Ceasing to be predatory in their habits, they became co- workers and found in fraternity, at once, the science of wealth and happiness. 'What shall I eat and drink, and wherewithal shall I be clothed?' stated as a problem beginning and ending in self, had been an anxious and an endless one. But when once it was conceived, not from the individual, but the fraternal standpoint, 'What shall we eat and drink, and wherewithal shall we be clothed?'—its difficulties vanished.

"Poverty with servitude had been the result, for the mass of humanity, of attempting to solve the problem of maintenance from the individual standpoint, but no sooner had the nation become the sole capitalist and employer than not alone did plenty replace poverty, but the last vestige of the serfdom of man to man disappeared from earth. Human slavery, so often vainly scotched, at last was killed. The means of subsistence no longer doled out by men to women, by employer to employed, by rich to poor, was distributed from a common stock as among children at the father's table. It was impossible for a man any longer to use his fellow men as tools for his own profit. His esteem was the only sort of gain he could thenceforth make out of him. There was no longer either arrogance or servility in the relations of human beings to one another. For the first time since the creation, every man stood up straight before God. The fear of want and the lust of gain became extinct motives when abundance was assured to all and immoderate possessions made impossible of attainment. There were no more beggars nor almoners. Equity left charity without an occupation. The Ten Commandments became well-nigh obsolete in a world where there was no temptation to theft, no occasion to lie either for fear or favor, no room for envy where all were equal, and little provocation to violence where men were disarmed of power to injure one another. Humanity's ancient dream of liberty, equality, fraternity, mocked by so many ages, at last was realized.

"As in the old society the generous, the just, the tender-hearted had been placed at a disadvantage by the possession of those qualities, so in the new society the cold-hearted, the greedy, and self-seeking found themselves out of joint with the world. Now that the conditions of life for the first time ceased to operate as a forcing process to develop the brutal

qualities of human nature, and the premium which had here-
tofore encouraged selfishness was not only removed but placed
upon unselfishness, it was for the first time possible to see
what unperverted human nature really was like. The depraved
tendencies, which had previously overgrown and obscured
the better to so large an extent, now withered like cellar fungi
in the open air, and the nobler qualities showed a sudden
luxuriance which turned cynics into panegyrists and for the
first time in human history tempted mankind to fall in love
with itself. Soon was fully revealed what the divines and
philosophers of the old world never would have believed—
that human nature in its essential qualities is good, not bad;
that men by their natural intention and structure are generous, not selfish; pitiful, not cruel; sympathetic, not arrogant;
godlike in aspirations, instinct with divinest impulses of
tenderness and self-sacrifice; images of God indeed, not the
travesties upon Him they had seemed. The constant pressure,
through numberless generations, of conditions of life which
might have perverted angels had not been able to essentially
alter the natural nobility of the stock, and these conditions
once removed, like a bent tree it had sprung back to its normal
uprightness.

"To put the whole matter in the nutshell of a parable, let
me compare humanity in the olden time to a rosebush planted
in a swamp, watered with black bog water, breathing mias-
matic fogs by day, and chilled with poison dews at night. Innumerable generations of gardeners had done their best to
make it bloom, but beyond an occasional half-opened bud
with a worm at the heart, their efforts had been unsuccessful.
Many, indeed, claimed that the bush was no rosebush at all,
but a noxious shrub, fit only to be uprooted and burned.
The gardeners for the most part, however, held that the bush
belonged to the rose family, but had some ineradicable taint
about it which prevented the buds from coming out, and ac-
counted for its generally sickly condition. There were a few,
indeed, who maintained that the stock was good enough, that
the trouble was in the bog, and that under more favorable

conditions the plant might be expected to do better. But these persons were not regular gardeners and, being condemned by the latter as mere theorists and daydreamers, were for the most part so regarded by the people. Moreover, urged some eminent moral philosophers, even conceding for the sake of the argument that the bush might possibly do better elsewhere, it was a more valuable discipline for the buds to try to bloom in a bog than it would be under more favorable conditions. The buds that succeeded in opening might indeed be very rare, and the flowers pale and scentless, but they represented far more moral effort than if they had bloomed spontaneously in a garden.

"The regular gardeners and the moral philosophers had their way. The bush remained rooted in the bog, and the old course of treatment went on. Continually new varieties of forcing mixtures were applied to the roots, and more recipes than could be numbered, each declared by its advocates the best and only suitable preparation, were used to kill the vermin and remove the mildew. This went on a very long time. Occasionally someone claimed to observe a slight improvement in the appearance of the bush, but there were quite as many who declared that it did not look so well as it used to. On the whole there could not be said to be any marked change. Finally, during a period of general despondency as to the prospects of the bush where it was, the idea of transplanting it was again mooted, and this time found favor. 'Let us try it,' was the general voice. 'Perhaps it may thrive better elsewhere, and here it is certainly doubtful if it be worth cultivating longer.' So it came about that the rosebush of humanity was transplanted and set in sweet, warm, dry earth, where the sun bathed it, the stars wooed it, and the south wind caressed it. Then it appeared that it was indeed a rosebush. The vermin and the mildew disappeared, and the bush was covered with most beautiful red roses, whose fragrance filled the world.

"It is a pledge of the destiny appointed for us that the Creator has set in our hearts an infinite standard of achievement, judged by which our past attainments seem always insignificant, and the goal never nearer. Had our forefathers conceived a state of society in which men should live together like brethren dwelling in unity, without strife or envying, violence or overreaching, and where, at the price of a degree of labor not greater than health demands, in their chosen occupations they should be wholly freed from care for the morrow and left with no more concern for their livelihood than trees which are watered by unfailing streams—had they conceived such a condition, I say, it would have seemed to them nothing less than paradise. They would have confounded it with their idea of heaven, nor dreamed that there could possibly lie further beyond anything to be desired or striven for.

"But how is it with us who stand on this height which they gazed up to? Already we have well-nigh forgotten, except when it is especially called to our minds by some occasion like the present, that it was not always with men as it is now. It is a strain on our imaginations to conceive the social arrangements of our immediate ancestors. We find them grotesque. The solution of the problem of physical maintenance so as to banish care and crime, so far from seeming to us an ultimate attainment, appears but as a preliminary to anything like real human progress. We have but relieved ourselves of an impertinent and needless harassment which hindered our ancestors from undertaking the real ends of existence. We are merely stripped for the race; no more. We are like a child which has just learned to stand upright and to walk. It is a great event, from the child's point of view, when he first walks. Perhaps he fancies that there can be little beyond that achievement, but a year later he has forgotten that he could not always walk. His horizon did but widen when he rose and enlarge as he moved. A great event indeed, in one sense, was his first step, but only as a beginning, not as the end. His true career was but then first entered on. The enfranchisement of humanity in the last century, from mental and physical absorption in working and scheming for the mere bodily necessities, may be regarded as a species of second birth of the race, without which its first birth to an existence that was but a burden would forever have remained unjustified, but whereby it is now abundantly vindicated. Since then, humanity has entered on a new phase of spiritual development, an evolution of higher faculties, the very existence of which in human nature our ancestors scarcely suspected. In place of the dreary hopelessness of the nineteenth century, its profound pessimism as to the future of humanity, the animating idea of the present age is an enthusiastic conception of the opportunities of our earthly existence and the unbounded possibilities of human nature. The betterment of mankind from generation to generation, physically, mentally, morally, is recognized as the one great object supremely worthy of effort and of sacrifice. We believe the race for the first time to have entered on the realization of God's ideal of it, and each generation must now be a step upward.

"Do you ask what we look for when unnumbered generations shall have passed away? I answer, the way stretches far before us, but the end is lost in light. For twofold is the return of man to God, 'Who is our home,' the return of the individual by the way of death, and the return of the race by the fulfillment of its evolution, when the divine secret hidden in the germ shall be perfectly unfolded. With a tear for the dark past, turn we then to the dazzling future and, veiling our eyes, press forward. The long and weary winter of the race is ended. Its summer has begun. Humanity has burst the chrysalis. The heavens are before it."

II. THE GILDED AGE
(1865-1888)

[THE REAL BOSTON] [1]

"Better take this right off, sir," he said, as I stared blankly at him. "You look kind of flushed, sir, and you need it."

I tossed off the liquor and began to realize what had happened to me. It was, of course, very plain. All that about the twentieth century had been a dream. I had but dreamed of that enlightened and carefree race of men and their ingeniously simple institutions, of the glorious new Boston with its domes and pinnacles, its gardens and fountains, and its universal reign of comfort. The amiable family which I had learned to know so well, my genial host and mentor, Dr. Leete, his wife, and their daughter, the . . . beauteous Edith, my betrothed—these, too, had been but figments of a vision.

For a considerable time I remained in the attitude in which this conviction had come over me, sitting up in bed gazing at vacancy, absorbed in recalling the scenes and incidents of my fantastic experience. Sawyer [my faithful servant] . . . was meanwhile anxiously inquiring what was the matter with me. Roused at length by his importunities to a recognition of my surroundings, I pulled myself together with an effort and assured the faithful fellow that I was all right. "I have had an extraordinary dream, that's all, Sawyer," I said, "a most-ex-traor-dinary-dream."

I dressed in a mechanical way, feeling light-headed and oddly uncertain of myself, and sat down to the coffee and rolls

[1] [From *Looking Backward,* Chapter XXVIII.]

which Sawyer was in the habit of providing for my refresh-
ment before I left the house. The morning newspaper lay by
the plate. I took it up, and my eye fell on the date, May 31,
1887. I had known, of course, from the moment I opened my
eyes that my long and detailed experience in another century
had been a dream, and yet it was startling to have it so con-
clusively demonstrated that the world was but a few hours
older than when I had lain down to sleep.

Glancing at the table of contents at the head of the paper,
which reviewed the news of the morning, I read the following summary:

FOREIGN AFFAIRS.—The impending war between France
and Germany. The French Chamber asked for new military
credits to meet Germany's increase of her army. Probability
that all Europe will be involved in case of war.—Great
suffering among the unemployed in London. They demand
work. Monster demonstration to be made. The authorities
uneasy.—Great strikes in Belgium. The government preparing to repress outbreaks. Shocking facts in regard to
the employment of girls in Belgian coal mines.—Wholesale evictions in Ireland.

HOME AFFAIRS.—The epidemic of fraud unchecked. Embezzlement of half a million in New York.—Misappropria-
tion of a trust fund by executors. Orphans left penniless.—
Clever system of thefts by a bank teller; $50,000 gone.—
The coal barons decide to advance the price of coal and
reduce production.—Speculators engineering a great wheat
corner at Chicago.—A clique forcing up the price of coffee.—
Enormous land-grabs of Western syndicates.—Revelations
of shocking corruption among Chicago officials. Systematic
bribery.—The trials of the Boodle aldermen to go on at
New York.—Large failures of business houses. Fears of a
business crisis.—A large grist of burglaries and larcenies.—
A woman murdered in cold blood for her money at New
Haven.—A householder shot by a burglar in this city last
night.—A man shoots himself in Worcester because he could

not get work. A large family left destitute.—An aged couple in New Jersey commit suicide rather than go to the poorhouse.—Pitiable destitution among the women wage workers in the great cities.—Startling growth of illiteracy in Massachusetts.—More insane asylums wanted.—Decoration Day addresses. Professor Brown's oration on the moral grandeur of nineteenth-century civilization.

It was indeed the nineteenth century to which I had awaked; there could be no kind of doubt about that. Its complete microcosm this summary of the day's news had presented, even to that last unmistakable touch of fatuous self-complacency. Coming after such a damning indictment of the age as that one day's chronicle of world-wide bloodshed, greed, and tyranny, was a bit of cynicism worthy of Mephistopheles, and yet of all whose eyes it had met this morning I was, perhaps, the only one who perceived the cynicism, and but yesterday I should have perceived it no more than the others. That strange dream it was which had made all the difference. For I know not how long, I forgot my surroundings after this and was again in fancy moving in that vivid dreamworld, in that glorious city, with its homes of simple comfort and its gorgeous public palaces. Around me were again faces unmarred by arrogance or servility, by envy or greed, by anxious care or feverish ambition; and stately forms of men and women who had never known fear of a fellow man or depended on his favor, but always, in the words of that sermon which still rang in my ears, had "stood up straight before God." [2]

With a profound sigh and a sense of irreparable loss, not the less poignant that it was a loss of what had never really been, I roused at last from my reverie and soon after left the house.

A dozen times between my door and Washington Street I had to stop and pull myself together, such power had been

[2] [See p. 53.]

in that vision of the Boston of the future to make the real
Boston strange. The squalor and malodorousness of the town
struck me, from the moment I stood upon the street, as facts
I had never before observed. But yesterday, moreover, it had
seemed quite a matter of course that some of my fellow
citizens should wear silks, and others rags; that some should
look well-fed, and others hungry. Now, on the contrary, the
glaring disparities in the dress and condition of the men and
women who brushed against each other on the sidewalks
shocked me at every step, and yet more the entire indifference
which the prosperous showed to the plight of the unfortunate.
Were these human beings, who could behold the wretchedness
of their fellows without so much as a change of countenance?
And yet, all the while, I knew well that it was I who had
changed, and not my contemporaries. I had dreamed of a
city whose people fared all alike as children of one family,
and were one another's keepers in all things.

Another feature of the real Boston, which assumed the
extraordinary effect of strangeness that marks familiar things
seen in a new light, was the prevalence of advertising. There
had been no personal advertising in the Boston of the
twentieth century, because there was no need of any, but here
the walls of the buildings, the windows, the broadsides of
the newspapers in every hand, the very pavements—everything in fact in sight, save the sky—were covered with the
appeals of individuals who sought, under innumerable pre-
texts, to attract the contributions of others to their support.
However the wording might vary, the tenor of all these appeals
was the same:

"Help John Jones. Never mind the rest. They are frauds.
I, John Jones, am the right one. Buy of me. Employ me.
Visit me. Hear me, John Jones. Look at me. Make no mistake,
John Jones is the man and nobody else. Let the rest starve,
but for God's sake remember John Jones!"

Whether the pathos or the moral repulsiveness of the
spectacle most impressed me, so suddenly become a stranger
in my own city, I know not. Wretched men, I was moved to

cry, who, because they will not learn to be helpers of one another, are doomed to be beggars of one another from the least to the greatest! This horrible babel of shameless self-assertion and mutual depreciation, this stunning clamor of conflicting boasts, appeals, and adjurations, this stupendous system of brazen beggary, what was it all but the necessity of a society in which the opportunity to serve the world according to his gifts, instead of being secured to every man as the first object of social organization, had to be fought for!

I reached Washington Street at the busiest point, and there I stood and laughed aloud, to the scandal of the passers-by. For my life I could not have helped it, with such a mad humor was I moved at sight of the interminable rows of stores on either side, up and down the street so far as I could see—scores of them, to make the spectacle more utterly preposterous, within a stone's throw devoted to selling the same sort of goods. Stores! stores! stores! miles of stores! ten thousand stores to distribute the goods needed by this one city, which in my dream had been supplied with all things from a single warehouse, as they were ordered through one great store in every quarter, where the buyer, without waste of time or labor, found under one roof the world's assortment in whatever line he desired. There the labor of distribution had been so slight as to add but a scarcely perceptible fraction to the cost of commodities to the user. The cost of production was virtually all he paid. But here the mere distribution of the goods, their handling alone, added a fourth, a third, a half and more, to the cost. All these ten thousand plants must be paid for, their rent, their staffs or superintendence, their platoons of salesmen, their ten thousand sets of accountants, jobbers, and business dependents, with all they spent in advertising themselves and fighting one another, and the consumers must do the paying. What a famous process for beggaring a nation!

Were these serious men I saw about me, or children, who did their business on such a plan? Could they be reasoning beings, who did not see the folly which, when the product is made and ready for use, wastes so much of it in getting it to the user? If people eat with a spoon that leaks half its contents between bowl and lip, are they not likely to go hungry?

I had passed through Washington Street thousands of times before and viewed the ways of those who sold merchandise, but my curiosity concerning them was as if I had never gone by their way before. I took wondering note of the show windows of the stores, filled with goods arranged with a wealth of pains and artistic device to attract the eye. I saw the throngs of ladies looking in, and the proprietors eagerly watching the effect of the bait. I went within and noted the hawk-eyed floorwalker watching for business, overlooking the clerks, keeping them up to their task of inducing the customers to buy, buy, buy; for money if they had it, for credit if they had it not, to buy what they wanted not, more than they wanted, what they could not afford. At times I momentarily lost the clue and was confused by the sight. Why this effort to induce people to buy? Surely that had nothing to do with the legitimate business of distributing products to those who needed them. Surely it was the sheerest waste to force upon people what they did not want, but what might be useful to another. The nation was so much the poorer for every such achievement. What were these clerks thinking of? Then I would remember that they were not acting as distributors like those in the store I had visited in the dream Boston. They were not serving the public interest, but their immediate personal interest, and it was nothing to them what the ultimate effect of their course on the general prosperity might be if but they increased their own hoard, for these goods were their own, and the more they sold and the more they got for them, the greater their gain. The more wasteful the people were, the more articles they did not want which they could be induced to buy, the better for these sellers. To encourage prodigality was the express aim of the ten thousand stores of Boston.

Nor were these storekeepers and clerks a whit worse men than any others in Boston. They must earn a living and sup-

port their families, and how were they to find a trade to do
it by which did not necessitate placing their individual interests before those of others and that of all? They could not
be asked to starve while they waited for an order of things
such as I had seen in my dream, in which the interest of each
and that of all were identical. But, God in heaven! What
wonder, under such a system as this about me—what wonder
that the city was so shabby, and the people so meanly dressed,
and so many of them ragged and hungry!

Some time after this it was that I drifted over into South
Boston and found myself among the manufacturing establishments. I had been in this quarter of the city a hundred times
before, just as I had been on Washington Street, but here,
as well as there, I now first perceived the true significance of
what I witnessed. Formerly I had taken pride in the fact that,
by actual count, Boston had some four thousand independent
manufacturing establishments; but in this very multiplicity
and independence I recognized now the secret of the insignificant total product of their industry.

If Washington Street had been like a lane in Bedlam, this
was a spectacle as much more melancholy as production is a
more vital function than distribution. For not only were
these four establishments not working in concert, and for
that reason alone operating at prodigious disadvantage, but,
as if this did not involve a sufficiently disastrous loss of power,
they were using their utmost skill to frustrate one another's
effort, praying by night and working by day for the destruction of one another's enterprises.

The roar and rattle of wheels and hammers resounding
from every side was not the hum of a peaceful industry, but
the clangor of swords wielded by foemen. These mills and
shops were so many forts, each under its own flag, its guns
trained on the mills and shops about it, and its sappers busy
below, undermining them.

Within each one of these forts the strictest organization of
industry was insisted on; the separate gangs worked under a
single central authority. No interference and no duplicating

of work were permitted. Each had his allotted task, and none was idle. By what hiatus in the logical faculty, by what lost link of reasoning [can you] account, then, for the failure to recognize the necessity of applying the same principle to the organization of the national industries as a whole, to see that if lack of organization could impair the efficiency of a shop, it must have effects as much more disastrous in disabling the industries of the nation at large, as the latter are vaster in volume and more complex in the relationship of their parts.

People would be prompt enough to ridicule an army in which there were neither companies, battalions, regiments, brigades, divisions, or army corps—no unit of organization, in fact, larger than the corporal's squad, with no officer higher than a corporal, and all the corporals equal in authority. And yet just such an army were the manufacturing industries of nineteenth-century Boston, an army of four thousand independent squads led by four thousand independent corporals, each with a separate plan of campaign.

Knots of idle men were to be seen here and there on every side, some idle because they could find no work at any price, others because they could not get what they thought a fair price.

I accosted some of the latter, and they told me their grievances. It was very little comfort I could give them. "I am sorry for you," I said. "You get little enough, certainly, and yet the wonder to me is, not that industries conducted as these are do not pay you living wages, but that they are able to pay you any wages at all."

Making my way back again after this to the peninsular city, toward three o'clock I stood on State Street, staring, as if I had never seen them before, at the banks and brokers' offices, and other financial institutions, of which there had been in the State Street of my vision no vestige. Businessmen, confidential clerks, and errand boys were thronging in and out of the banks, for it wanted but a few minutes of the closing hour. Opposite me was the bank where I did business, and presently I crossed the street, and, going in with the crowd, stood in a recess of the wall looking on at the army of clerks handling money, and the cues of depositors at the tellers' windows. An old gentleman whom I knew, a director of the bank, passing me and observing my contemplative attitude, stopped a moment.

"Interesting sight, isn't it, Mr. West," he said. "Wonderful piece of mechanism; I find it so myself. I like sometimes to stand and look on at it just as you are doing. It's a poem, sir, a poem, that's what I call it. Did you ever think, Mr. West, that the bank is the heart of the business system? From it and to it, in endless flux and reflux, the lifeblood goes. It is flowing in now. It will flow out again in the morning." And pleased with his little conceit, the old man passed on smiling.

Yesterday I should have considered the simile apt enough, but since then I had visited a world incomparably more affluent than this, in which money was unknown and without conceivable use. I had learned that it had a use in the world around me only because the work of producing the nation's livelihood, instead of being regarded as the most strictly public and common of all concerns, and as such conducted by the nation, was abandoned to the haphazard efforts of individuals. This original mistake necessitated endless exchanges to bring about any sort of general distribution of products. These exchanges money effected—how equitably, might be seen in a walk from the tenement house districts to the Back Bay—at the cost of an army of men taken from productive labor to manage it, with constant ruinous breakdowns of its machinery, and a generally debauching influence on mankind which had justified its description, from ancient time, as the "root of all evil."

Alas for the poor old bank director with his poem! He had mistaken the throbbing of an abscess for the beating of the heart. What he called "a wonderful piece of mechanism" was an imperfect device to remedy an unnecessary defect, the clumsy crutch of a self-made cripple.

After the banks had closed I wandered aimlessly about the business quarter for an hour or two, and later sat a while on one of the benches of the Common, finding an interest merely in watching the throngs that passed, such as one has in studying the populace of a foreign city, so strange since yesterday had my fellow citizens and their ways become to me. For thirty years I had lived among them, and yet I seemed to have never noted before how drawn and anxious were their faces, of the rich as of the poor, the refined, acute faces of the educated as well as the dull masks of the ignorant. And well it might be so, for I saw now, as never before I had seen so plainly, that each as he walked constantly turned to catch the whispers of a specter at his ear, the Specter of Uncertainty. "Do your work never so well," the specter was whispering, "rise early and toil till late, rob cunningly or serve faithfully, you shall never know security. Rich you may be now and still come to poverty at last. Leave never so much wealth to your children, you cannot buy the assurance that your son may not be the servant of your servant, or that your daughter will not have to sell herself for bread."

A man passing by thrust an advertising card in my hand, which set forth the merits of some new scheme of life insurance. The incident reminded me of the only device, pathetic in its admission of the universal need it so poorly supplied, which offered these tired and hunted men and women even a partial protection from uncertainty. By this means those already well-to-do, I remembered, might purchase a precarious confidence that after their death their loved ones would not, for a while at least, be trampled under the feet of men. But this was all, and this was only for those who could pay well for it. What idea was possible to these wretched dwellers in the land of Ishmael—where every man's hand was against each, and the hand of each against every other—of true life insurance as I had seen it among the people of that dreamland, each of whom, by virtue merely of his membership in the national family, was guaranteed against need of any sort by a policy underwritten by one hundred million fellow countrymen.

Some time after this it was that I recall a glimpse of myself standing on the steps of a building on Tremont Street,

looking at a military parade. A regiment was passing. It was
the first sight in that dreary day which had inspired me with
any other emotions than wondering pity and amazement.
Here at last were order and reason, an exhibition of what
intelligent co-operation can accomplish. The people who
stood looking on with kindling faces—could it be that the
sight had for them no more than a spectacular interest?
Could they fail to see that it was their perfect concert of
action, their organization under one control, which made
these men the tremendous engine they were, able to vanquish
a mob ten times as numerous? Seeing this so plainly, could
they fail to compare the scientific manner in which the
nation went to war with the unscientific manner in which it
went to work? Would they not query since what time the
killing of men had been a task so much more important than
feeding and clothing them, that a trained army should be
deemed alone adequate to the former, while the latter was
left to a mob?

It was now toward nightfall, and the streets were thronged
with the workers from the stores, the shops, and mills. Carried
along with the stronger part of the current, I found myself,
as it began to grow dark, in the midst of a scene of squalor
and human degradation such as only the South Cove tenement district could present. I had seen the mad wasting of
human labor; here I saw in direst shape the want that waste
had bred.

From the black doorways and windows of the rookeries on
every side came gusts of fetid air. The streets and alleys
reeked with the effluvia of a slave ship's between-decks. As I
passed I had glimpses within of pale babies gasping out their
lives amid sultry stenches, of hopeless-faced women deformed
by hardship, retaining of womanhood no trait save weakness, while from the windows leered girls with brows of brass.
Like the starving bands of mongrel curs that infest the streets
of Moslem towns, swarms of half-clad brutalized children
filled the air with shrieks and curses as they fought and
tumbled among the garbage that littered the courtyards.

There was nothing in all this that was new to me. Often

had I passed through this part of the city and witnessed its sights with feelings of disgust mingled with a certain philosophical wonder at the extremities mortals will endure, and still cling to life. But not alone as regarded the economical follies of this age, but equally as touched its moral abominations, scales had fallen from my eyes since that vision of another century. No more did I look upon the woeful dwellers in this inferno with a callous curiosity as creatures scarcely human. I saw in them my brothers and sisters, my parents, my children, flesh of my flesh, blood of my blood. The festering mass of human wretchedness about me offended not now my senses merely, but pierced my heart like a knife, so that I could not repress sighs and groans. I not only saw but felt in my body all that I saw.

Presently, too, as I observed the wretched beings about me more closely, I perceived that they were all quite dead. Their bodies were so many living sepulchers. On each brutal brow was plainly written the *hic jacet* [epitaph] of a soul dead within.

As I looked, horror-struck, from one death's head to another, I was affected by a singular hallucination. Like a wavering translucent spirit face superimposed upon each of these brutish masks I saw the ideal, the possible face that would have been the actual if mind and soul had lived. It was not till I was aware of these ghostly faces, and of the reproach that could not be gainsaid which was in their eyes, that the full piteousness of the ruin that had been wrought was revealed to me. I was moved with contrition as with a strong agony, for I had been one of those who had endured that these things should be. I had been one of those who, well knowing that they were, had not desired to hear or be compelled to think much of them, but had gone on as if they were not, seeking my own pleasure and profit. Therefore now I found upon my garments the blood of this great multitude of strangled souls of my brothers. The voice of their blood cried out against me from the ground. Every stone of the reeking pavements, every brick of the pestilential rookeries, found a tongue and called after me as I fled: "What hast thou done with thy brother Abel?"

I have no clear recollection of anything after this till I found myself standing on the carved stone steps of the magnificent home of my betrothed on Commonwealth Avenue. Amid the tumult of my thoughts that day, I had scarcely once thought of her, but now obeying some unconscious impulse my feet had found the familiar way to her door. I was told that the family were at dinner, but word was sent out that I should join them at table. Besides the family, I found several guests present, all known to me. The table glittered with plates and costly china. The ladies were sumptuously dressed and wore the jewels of queens. The scene was one of costly elegance and lavish luxury. The company was in excellent spirits, and there was plentiful laughter and a running fire of jests.

To me it was as if, in wandering through the place of doom, my blood turned to tears by its sights, and my spirit attuned to sorrow, pity, and despair, I had happened in some glade upon a merry party of roisterers. I sat in silence until Edith began to rally me upon my somber looks. What ailed me? The others presently joined in the playful assault, and I became a target for quips and jests. Where had I been, and what had I seen to make such a dull fellow of me?

"I have been in Golgotha," at last I answered. "I have seen Humanity hanging on a cross! Do none of you know what sights the sun and stars look down on in this city, that you can think and talk of anything else? Do you not know that close to your doors a great multitude of men and women, flesh of your flesh, live lives that are one agony from birth to death? Listen! Their dwellings are so near that if you hush your laughter you will hear their grievous voices, the piteous crying of the little ones that suckle poverty, the hoarse curses of men sodden in misery turned halfway back to brutes, the chaffering of an army of women selling themselves for bread. With what have you stopped your ears that you do not hear these doleful sounds? For me, I can hear nothing else."

Silence followed my words. A passion of pity had shaken me as I spoke, but when I looked around upon the company I saw that, far from being stirred as I was, their faces expressed a cold and hard astonishment, mingled in Edith's with extreme mortification, in her father's with anger. The ladies were exchanging scandalized looks, while one of the gentlemen had put up his eyeglass and was studying me with an air of scientific curiosity. When I saw that things which were to me so intolerable moved them not at all, that words that melted my heart to speak had only offended them with the speaker, I was at first stunned, and then overcome with a desperate sickness and faintness at the heart. What hope was there for the wretched, for the world, if thoughtful men and tender women were not moved by things like these! Then I bethought myself that it must be because I had not spoken aright. No doubt I had put the case badly. They were angry because they thought I was berating them, when God knew I was merely thinking of the horror of the fact without any attempt to assign the responsibility for it.

I restrained my passion, and tried to speak calmly and logically that I might correct this impression. I told them that I had not meant to accuse them, as if they, or the rich in general, were responsible for the misery of the world. True indeed it was, that the superfluity which they wasted would, otherwise bestowed, relieve much bitter suffering. These costly viands, these rich wines, these gorgeous fabrics and glistening jewels represented the ransom of many lives. They were verily not without the guiltiness of those who waste in a land stricken with famine. Nevertheless, all the waste of all the rich, were it saved, would go but a little way to cure the poverty of the world. There was so little to divide that even if the rich went share and share with the poor, there would be but a common fare of crusts, albeit made very sweet then by brotherly love.

The folly of men, not their hardheartedness, was the great cause of the world's poverty. It was not the crime of man, nor of any class of men, that made the race so miserable, but a hideous, ghastly mistake, a colossal world-darkening blunder. And then I showed them how four-fifths of the labor of men was utterly wasted by the mutual warfare, the lack of organization and concert among the workers. Seeking to make the matter very plain, I instanced the case of arid lands where the soil yielded the means of life only by careful use of the watercourses for irrigation. I showed how in such countries it was counted the most important function of the government to see that the water was not wasted by the selfishness or ignorance of individuals, since otherwise there would be famine. To this end its use was strictly regulated and systematized, and individuals of their mere caprice were not permitted to dam it or divert it, or in any way to tamper with it.

The labor of men, I explained, was the fertilizing stream which alone rendered earth habitable. It was but a scanty stream at best, and its use required to be regulated by a system which expended every drop to the best advantage, if the world were to be supported in abundance. But how far from any system was the actual practice! Every man wasted the precious fluid as he wished, animated only by the equal motives of saving his own crop and spoiling his neighbor's, that his might sell the better. What with greed and what with spite some fields were flooded while others were parched, and half the water ran wholly to waste. In such a land, though a few by strength or cunning might win the means of luxury, the lot of the great mass must be poverty, and of the weak and ignorant bitter want and perennial famine.

Let but the famine-stricken nation assume the function it had neglected, and regulate for the common good the course of the life-giving stream, and the earth would bloom like one garden, and none of its children lack any good thing. I described the physical felicity, mental enlightenment, and moral elevation which would then attend the lives of all men. With fervency I spoke of that new world, blessed with plenty, purified by justice and sweetened by brotherly kindness, the world of which I had indeed but dreamed, but which might so easily be made real. But when I had expected now surely the faces around me to light up with emotions akin to mine, they grew ever more dark, angry, and scornful. Instead of enthusiasm, the ladies showed only aversion and dread, while the men interrupted me with shouts of reprobation and contempt. "Madman!" "Pestilent fellow!" "Fanatic!" "Enemy of society!" were some of their cries, and the one who had before taken his eyeglass to me, exclaimed, "He says we are to have no more poor. Ha! ha!"

"Put the fellow out!" exclaimed the father of my betrothed, and at the signal the men sprang from their chairs and advanced upon me.

[A STAGECOACH] [1]

By way of attempting to give the reader some general impression of the way people lived together in those days [the late nineteenth century], and especially of the relations of the rich and poor to one another, perhaps I cannot do better than to compare society as it then was to a prodigious coach which the masses of humanity were harnessed to and dragged toilsomely along a very hilly and sandy road. The driver was hunger, and permitted no lagging, though the pace was necessarily very slow. Despite the difficulty of drawing the coach at all along so hard a road, the top was covered with passengers who never got down, even at the steepest ascents. These seats on top were very breezy and comfortable. Well up out of the dust, their occupants could enjoy the scenery at their leisure, or critically discuss the merits of the straining team. Naturally such places were in great demand and the competition for them was keen, everyone seeking as the first end in life to secure a seat on the coach for himself and to leave it to his child after him. By the rule of the coach a man could leave his seat to whom he wished, but on the other hand there were many accidents by which it might at any time be wholly lost. For all that they were so easy, the seats were very in-

[1] [From *Looking Backward*, Chapter I.]

secure, and at every sudden jolt of the coach persons were slipping out of them and falling to the ground, where they were instantly compelled to take hold of the rope and help to drag the coach on which they had before ridden so pleasantly. It was naturally regarded as a terrible misfortune to lose one's seat, and the apprehension that this might happen to them or their friends was a constant cloud upon the happiness of those who rode.

But did they think only of themselves, you ask. Was not their very luxury rendered intolerable to them by comparison with the lot of their brothers and sisters in the harness, and the knowledge that their own weight added to their toil? Had they no compassion for fellow beings from whom fortune only distinguished them? Oh, yes; commiseration was frequently expressed by those who rode for those who had to pull the coach, especially when the vehicle came to a bad place in the road, as it was constantly doing, or to a particularly steep hill. At such times, the desperate straining of the team, their agonized leaping and plunging under the pitiless lashing of hunger, the many who fainted at the rope and were trampled in the mire, made a very distressing spectacle, which often called forth highly creditable displays of feeling on the top of the coach. At such times the passengers would call down encouragingly to the toilers of the rope, exhorting them to patience and holding out hopes of possible compensation in another world for the hardness of their lot, while others contributed to buy salves and liniments for the crippled and injured. It was agreed that it was a great pity that the coach should be so hard to pull, and there was a sense of general relief when the specially bad piece of road was gotten over. This relief was not, indeed, wholly on account of the team, for there was always some danger at these bad places of a general overturn in which all would lose their seats.

It must in truth be admitted that the main effect of the spectacle of the misery of the toilers at the rope was to enhance the passengers' sense of the value of their seats upon the coach and to cause them to hold on to them more desperately than before. If the passengers could only have felt assured that neither they nor their friends would ever fall from the top, it is probable that, beyond contributing to the funds for liniments and bandages, they would have troubled themselves extremely little about those who dragged the coach.

I am well aware that this will appear to the men and women of the twentieth century an incredible inhumanity, but there are two facts, both very curious, which partly explain it. In the first place, it was firmly and sincerely believed that there was no other way in which Society could get along, except the many pulled at the rope and the few rode, and not only this, but that no very radical improvement even was possible, either in the harness, the coach, the roadway, or the distribution of the toil. It had always been as it was, and it always would be so. It was a pity, but it could not be helped, and philosophy forbade wasting compassion on what was beyond remedy.

The other fact is yet more curious, consisting in a singular hallucination which those on the top of the coach generally shared, that they were not exactly like their brothers and sisters who pulled at the rope, but of finer clay, in some way belonging to a higher order of beings who might justly expect to be drawn. This seems unaccountable, but, as I once rode on this very coach and shared that very hallucination, I ought to be believed. The strangest thing about the hallucination was that those who had but just climbed up from the ground, before they had outgrown the marks of the rope upon their hands, began to fall under its influence. As for those whose parents and grandparents before them had been so fortunate as to keep their seats on the top, the conviction they cherished of the essential difference between their sort of humanity and the common article was absolute. The effect of such a delusion in moderating fellow feeling for the sufferings of the mass of men into a distant and philosophical compassion is obvious. To it I refer as the only extenuation I can offer for the indifference which, at the period I write of, marked my own attitude toward the misery of my brothers.

[INDUSTRIAL STRIFE] [1]

Presently, as we were crossing Boston Common, absorbed in conversation, a shadow fell athwart the way, and looking up, I saw towering above us a sculptured group of heroic size.

"Who are these?" I exclaimed.

"You ought to know, if anyone," said the doctor. "They are contemporaries of yours who were making a good deal of disturbance in your day."

But, indeed, it had only been as an involuntary expression of surprise that I had questioned what the figures stood for.

Let me tell you, readers of the twentieth century, what I saw up there on the pedestal, and you will recognize the world-famous group. Shoulder to shoulder, as if rallied to resist assault, were three figures of men in the garb of the laboring class of my time. They were bareheaded, and their coarse-textured shirts, rolled above the elbow and open at the breast, showed the sinewy arms and chest. Before them, on the ground, lay a pair of shovels and a pickax. The central figure, with the right hand extended palm outward, was pointing to the discarded tools. The arms of the other two were folded on their breasts. The faces were coarse and hard in outline and bristled with unkempt beards. Their expression was one of dogged defiance, and their gaze was fixed with such scowling intensity upon the void space before them that I involuntarily glanced behind me to see what they were looking at. There were two women also in the group, as coarse of dress and features as the men. One was kneeling before the figure on the right, holding up to him with one arm an emaciated, half-clad infant, while with the other she indicated the implements at his feet with an imploring gesture. The second of the women was plucking by the sleeve the man on

1 [From *Equality*, Chapter XXV.]

the left as if to draw him back, while with the other hand she covered her eyes. But the men heeded the women not at all, nor seemed, in their bitter wrath, to know that they were there.

[THE MASTERS OF THE BREAD] [1]

. . . Everywhere men, women, and children stood in the market place crying to the Masters of the Bread to take them to be their servants, that they might have bread. The strong men said: "O Lords of the Bread, feel our thews and sinews, our arms and our legs; see how strong we are. Take us and use us. Let us dig for you. Let us hew for you. Let us go down in the mine and delve for you. Let us freeze and starve in the forecastles of your ships. Send us into the hells of your steamship stokeholes. Do what you will with us, but let us serve you, that we may eat and not die!"

Then spoke up also the learned men, the scribes and the lawyers, whose strength was in their brains and not in their bodies: "O Masters of the Bread," they said, "take us to be your servants and to do your will. See how fine is our wit, how great our knowledge; our minds are stored with the treasures of learning and the subtlety of all the philosophies. To us has been given clearer vision than to others, and the power of persuasion that we should be leaders of the people, voices to the voiceless, and eyes to the blind. But the people whom we should serve have no bread to give us. Therefore, Masters of the Bread, give us to eat, and we will betray the people to you, for we must live. We will plead for you in the courts against the widow and the fatherless. We will speak and write in your praise, and with cunning words confound those who speak against you and your power and

1 [From *Equality*, Chapter XIV.]

state. And nothing that you require of us shall seem too much. But because we sell not only our bodies, but our souls also, give us more bread than these laborers receive, who sell their bodies only."

And the priests and Levites also cried out as the Lords of the Bread passed through the market place: "Take us, Masters, to be your servants and to do your will, for we also must eat, and only you have the bread. We are the guardians of the sacred oracles, and the people hearken unto us and reply not, for our voice to them is as the voice of God. But we must have bread to eat like others. Give us therefore plentifully of your bread, and we will speak to the people, that they be still and trouble you not with their murmurings because of hunger. In the name of God the Father will we forbid them to claim the rights of brothers, and in the name of the Prince of Peace will we preach your law of competition."

And above all the clamor of the men were heard the voices of a multitude of women crying to the Masters of the Bread: "Pass us not by, for we also must eat. The men are stronger than we, but they eat much bread while we eat little, so that though we be not so strong, yet in the end you shall not lose if you take us to be your servants instead of them. And if you will not take us for our labor's sake, yet look upon us; we are women, and should be fair in your eyes. Take us and do with us according to your pleasure, for we must eat."

And above all the chaffering of the market, the hoarse voices of the men, and the shrill voices of the women, rose the piping treble of the little children, crying: "Take us to be your servants, for the breasts of our mothers are dry, and our fathers have no bread for us, and we hunger. We are weak, indeed, but we ask so little, so very little, that at last we shall be cheaper to you than the men, our fathers, who eat so much, and the women, our mothers, who eat more than we."

And the Masters of the Bread, having taken for their use or pleasure such of the men, the women, and the little ones as they saw fit, passed by. And there was left a great multitude in the market place for whom there was no bread.

[THE BURDEN OF GUILT] [1]

"I am fond of speculating what sort of a world, morally speaking, we should have if there were no memory. One thing is clear, we should have no such very wicked people as we have now. . . . Memory is the principle of moral degeneration. Remembered sin is the most utterly diabolical influence in the universe. It invariably either debauches or martyrizes men and women, accordingly as it renders them desperate and hardened, or makes them a prey to undying grief and self-contempt. When I consider that more sin is the only anodyne for sin, and that the only way to cure the ache of conscience is to harden it, I marvel that even so many as do, essay the bitter and hopeless way of repentance and reform. In the main, the pangs of conscience, so much vaunted by some, do most certainly drive ten people deeper into sin where they bring one back to virtue."

"But," remarked Henry, "suppose there were no memory, and men did forget their acts, they would remain just as responsible for them as now."

"Precisely; that is, not at all," replied the doctor.

"You don't mean to say there is no such thing as responsibility, no such thing as justice? Oh, I see, you deny free will. You are a necessitarian."

The doctor waved his hand rather contemptuously.

"I know nothing about your theological distinctions: I am a doctor. I say that there is no such thing as moral responsibility for past acts, no such thing as real justice in punishing them, for the reason that human beings are not stationary existences, but changing, growing, incessantly progressive organisms, which in no two moments are the same. Therefore justice, whose only possible mode of proceeding is to punish in present time for what is done in past time, must always

1 [From *Dr. Heidenhoff's Process,* Chapters X and XI.]

punish a person more or less similar to, but never identical with, the one who committed the offense, and therein must be no justice.

"Why sir, it is no theory of mine, but the testimony of universal consciousness, if you interrogate it aright, that the difference between the past and present selves of the same individual is so great as to make them different persons for all moral purposes. That single fact . . . that no man would care for vengeance on one who had injured him, provided he knew that all memory of the offense had been blotted utterly from his enemy's mind—proves the entire proposition. It shows that it is not the present self of his enemy that the avenger is angry with at all, but the past self. Even in the blindness of his wrath he intuitively recognizes the distinction between the two. He only hates the present man, and seeks vengeance on him in so far as he thinks that he exults in remembering the injury his past self did, or, if he does not exult, that he insults and humiliates him by the bare fact of remembering it. That is the continuing offense which alone keeps alive the avenger's wrath against him. His fault is not that he did the injury, for *he* did not do it, but that he remembers it.

"It is the first principle of justice, isn't it, that nobody ought to be punished for what he can't help? Can the man of today prevent or affect what he did yesterday; let me say, rather, what the man did out of whom he has grown—has grown, I repeat, by a physical process which he could not check save by suicide? As well punish him for Adam's sin, for he might as easily have prevented that, and is every whit as accountable for it. You pity the child born, without his choice, of depraved parents. Pity the man himself, the man of today who, by a process as inevitable as the child's birth, has grown on the rotten stock of yesterday. Think you, that it is not sometimes with a sense of loathing and horror unutterable, that he feels his fresh life thus inexorably knitting itself on, growing on, to that old stem? For, mind you well, the consciousness of the man exists alone in the present day and moment. There alone he lives. That is himself. The former days are his dead, for whose sins, in which he had no part, which perchance by his choice never would have been done, he is held to answer for, and to do penance. And you thought, young man, that there was such a thing as justice!"

"I can see," said Henry after a pause, "that when half a lifetime has intervened between a crime and its punishment, and the man has reformed, there is a certain lack of identity. I have always thought punishments in such cases very barbarous. I know that I should think it hard to answer for what I may have done as a boy, twenty years ago."

"Yes," said the doctor, "flagrant cases of that sort take the general eye, and people say that they are instances of retribution rather than justice. The unlikeness between the extremes of life, as between the babe and the man, the lad and the dotard, strikes every mind, and all admit that there is not any apparent identity between these widely parted points in the progress of a human organism. How then? How soon does identity begin to decay, and when is it gone—in one year, five years, ten years, twenty years, or how many? Shall we fix fifty years as the period of a moral statute of limitation, after which punishment shall be deemed barbarous? No, no. The gulf between the man of this instant and the man of the last is just as impassable as that between the babe and the man. What is past is eternally past. So far as the essence of justice is concerned, there is no difference between one of the cases of punishment which you called barbarous, and one in which the penalty follows the offense within the hour. There is no way of joining the past with the present, and there is no difference between what is a moment past and what is eternally past."

"Then the assassin as he withdraws the stiletto from his victim's breast is not the same man who plunged it in?"

"Obviously not," replied the doctor. "He may be exulting in the deed, or, more likely, he may be in a reaction of regret. He may be worse, he may be better. His being better or worse makes it neither more nor less just to punish him, though it may make it more or less expedient. Justice demands identity;

similarity, however close, will not answer. Though a mother could not tell her twin sons apart, it would not make it any more just to punish one for the other's sins."

"Then you don't believe in the punishment of crime?" said Henry.

"Most emphatically I do," replied the doctor; "only I don't believe in calling it justice or ascribing [to] it a moral significance. The punishment of criminals is a matter of public policy and expediency, precisely like measures for the suppression of nuisances or the prevention of epidemics. It is needful to restrain those who by crime have revealed their likelihood to commit further crimes, and to furnish by their punishment a motive to deter others from crime."

"And to deter the criminal himself after his release," added Henry.

"I included him in the word 'others,' " said the doctor. "The man who is punished is other from the man who did the act, and after punishment he is still other."

"Really, Doctor," observed Henry, "I don't see that a man who fully believes your theory is in any need of your process for obliterating his sins. He won't think of blaming himself for them anyway."

"True," said the doctor, "perfectly true. My process is for those who cannot attain to my philosophy. I break for the weak the chain of memory which holds them to the past; but stronger souls are independent of me. They can unloose the iron links and free themselves. Would that more had the needful wisdom and strength thus serenely to put their past behind them, leaving the dead to bury their dead, and go blithely forward, taking each new day as a life by itself, and reckoning themselves daily newborn, even as verily they are! Physically, mentally, indeed, the present must be forever the outgrowth of the past, conform to its conditions, bear its burdens; but moral responsibility for the past the present has none, and by the very definition of the words can have none. There is no need to tell people that they ought to regret and grieve over the errors of the past. They can't help doing that. I myself suffer at times pretty sharply from twinges of the rheumatism which I owe to youthful dissipation. It would be absurd enough for me, a quiet old fellow of sixty, to take blame to myself for what the wild student did, but, all the same, I confoundedly wish he hadn't.

"Ah, me!" continued the doctor. "Are there not sorrow and wrong enough in the present world without having moralists teach us that it is our duty to perpetuate all our past sins and shames in the multiplying mirror of memory, as if, forsooth, we were any more the causers of the sins of our past selves than of our fathers' sins? How many a man and woman have poisoned their lives with tears for some one sin far away in the past! . . .

"Remorse and shame and wan regret have wielded their cruel scepters over human lives, from the beginning until now. . . .

"The deeper the repentance, the more intense the longing and love for better things, the more poignant the pang of regret and the sense of irreparable loss. There is no sense, no end, no use in this law which increases the severity of the punishment as the victim grows in innocence. . . . Macbeth's question, 'Canst thou not minister to a mind diseased; pluck from the memory a rooted sorrow; raze out the written troubles of the brain?' was a puzzler to the sixteenth-century doctor, but he of the twentieth, yes, perhaps of the nineteenth, will be able to answer it affirmatively."

III. A REPUBLIC OF THE GOLDEN RULE

[THE GREAT TRUST] [1]

When in the course of the evening the ladies retired, leaving Dr. Leete and myself alone, he sounded me as to my disposition for sleep, saying that if I felt like it my bed was ready for me; but if I was inclined to wakefulness nothing would please him better than to bear me company. "I am a late bird myself," he said, "and, without suspicion of flattery, I may say that a companion more interesting than yourself could scarcely be imagined. It is decidedly not often that one has a chance to converse with a man of the nineteenth century."

Now I had been looking forward all evening with some dread to the time when I should be alone on retiring for the night. Surrounded by these most friendly strangers, stimulated and supported by their sympathetic interest, I had been able to keep my mental balance. Even then, however, in pauses of the conversation I had had glimpses, vivid as lightning flashes, of the horror of strangeness that was waiting to be faced when I could no longer command diversion. I knew I could not sleep that night, and as for lying awake and thinking, it argues no cowardice, I am sure, to confess that I was afraid of it. When, in reply to my host's question, I frankly told him this, he replied that it would be strange if I did not feel just so, but that I need have no anxiety about sleeping; whenever I wanted to go to bed, he would give me

[1] [*Looking Backward,* Chapter V.]

a dose which would insure me a sound night's sleep without fail. Next morning, no doubt, I would awake with the
feeling of an old citizen.

"Before I acquire that," I replied, "I must know a little
more about the sort of Boston I have come back to. You told
me when we were upon the housetop that though a century
only had elapsed since I fell asleep, it had been marked by
greater changes in the conditions of humanity than many a
previous millennium. With the city before me I could well
believe that, but I am very curious to know what some of the
changes have been. To make a beginning somewhere, for the
subject is doubtless a large one, what solution, if any, have
you found for the labor question? It was the Sphinx's riddle
of the nineteenth century, and when I dropped out, the
Sphinx was threatening to devour society because the answer
was not forthcoming. It is well worth sleeping a hundred
years to learn what the right answer was, if, indeed, you have
found it yet."

"As no such thing as the labor question is known nowadays," replied Dr. Leete, "and there is no way in which it
could arise, I suppose we may claim to have solved it. Society
would indeed have fully deserved being devoured if it had
failed to answer a riddle so entirely simple. In fact, to speak
by the book, it was not necessary for society to solve the riddle
at all. It may be said to have solved itself. The solution came
as the result of a process of industrial evolution which could
not have terminated otherwise. All that society had to do was
to recognize and co-operate with that evolution, when its
tendency had become unmistakable."

"I can only say," I answered, "that at the time I fell asleep
no such evolution had been recognized."

"It was in 1887 that you fell into this sleep, I think you
said."

"Yes, May 30th, 1887."

My companion regarded me musingly for some moments.
Then he observed, "And you tell me that even then there was
no general recognition of the nature of the crisis which so-

ciety was nearing? Of course, I fully credit your statement. The singular blindness of your contemporaries to the signs of the times is a phenomenon commented on by many of our historians, but few facts of history are more difficult for us to realize, so obvious and unmistakable as we look back seem the indications, which must also have come under your eyes, of the transformation about to come to pass. I should be interested, Mr. West, if you would give me a little more definite idea of the view which you and men of your grade of intellect took of the state and prospects of society in 1887. You must at least have realized that the widespread industrial and social troubles, and the underlying dissatisfaction of all classes with the inequalities of society, and the general misery of mankind, were portents of great changes of some sort."

"We did, indeed, fully realize that," I replied. "We felt that society was dragging anchor and in danger of going adrift. Whither it would drift nobody could say, but all feared the rocks."

"Nevertheless," said Dr. Leete, "the set of the current was perfectly perceptible if you had but taken pains to observe it, and it was not toward the rocks, but toward a deeper channel."

"We had a popular proverb," I replied, "that 'hindsight is better than foresight,' the force of which I shall now, no doubt, appreciate more fully than ever. All I can say is, that the prospect was such when I went into that long sleep that I should not have been surprised had I looked down from your housetop today on a heap of charred and moss-grown ruins instead of this glorious city."

Dr. Leete had listened to me with close attention and nodded thoughtfully as I finished speaking. "What you have said," he observed, "will be regarded as a most valuable vindication of Storiot, whose account of your era has been generally thought exaggerated in its picture of the gloom and confusion of men's minds. That a period of transition like that should be full of excitement and agitation was indeed to be looked for; but seeing how plain was the tendency of the forces in operation, it was natural to believe that hope rather than fear would have been the prevailing temper of the popular mind."

"You have not yet told me what was the answer to the riddle which you found," I said. "I am impatient to know by what contradiction of natural sequence the peace and prosperity which you now seem to enjoy could have been the outcome of an era like my own."

. . . "Since you are in the humor to talk rather than to sleep, as I certainly am, perhaps I cannot do better than to try to give you enough idea of our modern industrial system to dissipate at least the impression that there is any mystery about the process of its evolution. The Bostonians of your day had the reputation of being great askers of questions, and I am going to show my descent by asking you one to begin with. What should you name as the most prominent feature of the labor troubles of your day?"

"Why, the strikes, of course," I replied.

"Exactly, but what made the strikes so formidable?"

"The great labor organizations."

"And what was the motive of these great organizations?"

"The workmen claimed they had to organize to get their rights from the big corporations," I replied.

"That is just it," said Dr. Leete, "the organization of labor and the strikes were an effect, merely, of the concentration of capital in greater masses than had ever been known before. Before this concentration began, while as yet commerce and industry were conducted by innumerable petty concerns with small capital, instead of a small number of great concerns with vast capital, the individual workman was relatively important and independent in his relations to the employer. Moreover, when a little capital or a new idea was enough to start a man in business for himself, workingmen were constantly becoming employers, and there was no hard and fast line between the two classes. Labor unions were needless then, and general strikes out of the question. But when the era of small concerns with small capital was succeeded by that of the great aggregations of capital, all this was changed. The individual laborer, who had been relatively important to the small employer, was reduced to insignificance and powerlessness over against the great corporation, while at the same time the way upward to the grade of employer was closed to him. Self-defense drove him to union with his fellows.

"The records of the period show that the outcry against the concentration of capital was furious. Men believed that it threatened society with a form of tyranny more abhorrent than it had ever endured. They believed that the great corporations were preparing for them the yoke of a baser servitude than had ever been imposed on the race, servitude not to men but to soulless machines incapable of any motive but insatiable greed. Looking back, we cannot wonder at their desperation, for certainly humanity was never confronted with a fate more sordid and hideous than would have been the era of corporate tyranny which they anticipated.

"Meanwhile, without being in the smallest degree checked by the clamor against it, the absorption of business by ever larger monopolies continued. In the United States, where this tendency was later in developing than in Europe, there was not, after the beginning of the last quarter of the century, any opportunity whatever for individual enterprise in any important field of industry, unless backed by great capital. During the last decade of the century, such small businesses as still remained were fast-failing survivals of a past epoch or mere parasites on the great corporations, or else existed in fields too small to attract the great capitalists. Small businesses, as far as they still remained, were reduced to the condition of rats and mice, living in holes and corners, and counting on evading notice for the enjoyment of existence. The railroads had gone on combining till a few great syndicates controlled every rail in the land. In manufactories, every important staple was controlled by a syndicate. These syndicates, pools, trusts, or whatever their name, fixed prices and crushed all competition except when combinations as vast as themselves arose. Then a struggle, resulting in a still greater consolidation, ensued. The great city bazaar crushed its country rivals with branch stores, and in the city itself absorbed its smaller rivals till the business of a whole quarter was concentrated under one roof, with a hundred former proprietors of shops serving as clerks. Having no business of his own to put his money in, the small capitalist, at the same time that he took service under the corporation, found no other investment for his money but its stocks and bonds, thus becoming doubly dependent upon it.

"The fact that the desperate popular opposition to the consolidation of business in a few powerful hands had no effect to check it, proves that there must have been a strong economical reason for it. The small capitalists, with their innumerable petty concerns, had in fact yielded the field to the great aggregations of capital, because they belonged to a day of small things and were totally incompetent to the demands of an age of steam and telegraphs and the gigantic scale of its enterprises. To restore the former order of things, even if possible, would have involved returning to the day of stage-coaches. Oppressive and intolerable as was the regime of the great consolidations of capital, even its victims, while they cursed it, were forced to admit the prodigious increase of efficiency which had been imparted to the national industries, the vast economies effected by concentration of management and unity of organization, and to confess that since the new system had taken the place of the old, the wealth of the world had increased at a rate before undreamed of. To be sure, this vast increase had gone chiefly to make the rich richer, increasing the gap between them and the poor; but the fact remained that, as a means merely of producing wealth, capital had been proved efficient in proportion to its consolidation. The restoration of the old system with the subdivision of capital, if it were possible, might indeed bring back a greater equality of conditions with more individual dignity and freedom, but it would be at the price of general poverty and the arrest of material progress.

"Was there, then, no way of commanding the services of

the mighty wealth-producing principle of consolidated capital, without bowing down to a plutocracy like that of Carthage? As soon as men began to ask themselves these questions, they found the answer ready for them. The movement toward the conduct of business by larger and larger aggregations of capital, the tendency toward monopolies, which had been so desperately and vainly resisted, was recognized at last, in its true significance, as a process which only needed to complete its logical evolution to open a golden future to humanity.

"Early in the last century the evolution was completed by the final consolidation of the entire capital of the nation. The industry and commerce of the country, ceasing to be conducted by a set of irresponsible corporations and syndicates of private persons at their caprice and for their profit, were entrusted to a single syndicate representing the people, to be conducted in the common interest for the common profit. The nation, that is to say, organized as the one great business corporation in which all other corporations were absorbed; it became the one capitalist in the place of all other capitalists, the sole employer, the final monopoly in which all previous and lesser monopolies were swallowed up, a monopoly in the profits and economies of which all citizens shared. The epoch of trusts had ended in The Great Trust. In a word, the people of the United States concluded to assume the conduct of their own business, just as one hundred-odd years before they had assumed the conduct of their own government, organizing now for industrial purposes on precisely the same grounds that they had then organized for political purposes. At last, strangely late in the world's history, the obvious fact was perceived that no business is so essentially the public business as the industry and commerce on which the people's livelihood depends, and that to entrust it to private persons to be managed for private profit is a folly similar in kind, though vastly greater in magnitude, to that of surrendering the functions of political government to kings and nobles to be conducted for their personal glorification."

"Such a stupendous change as you describe," said I, "did

not, of course, take place without great bloodshed and terrible convulsions."

"On the contrary," replied Dr. Leete, "there was absolutely no violence. The change had been long foreseen. Public opinion had become fully ripe for it, and the whole mass of the people was behind it. There was no more possibility of opposing it by force than by argument. On the other hand, the popular sentiment toward the great corporations and those identified with them had ceased to be one of bitterness, as they came to realize their necessity as a link, a transition phase, in the evolution of the true industrial system. The most violent foes of the great private monopolies were now forced to recognize how invaluable and indispensable had been their office in educating the people up to the point of assuming control of their own business. Fifty years before, the consolidation of the industries of the country under national control would have seemed a very daring experiment to the most sanguine. But by a series of object lessons, seen and studied by all men, the great corporations had taught the people an entirely new set of ideas on this subject. They had seen for many years syndicates handling revenues greater than those of states, and directing the labors of hundreds of thousands of men with an efficiency and economy unattainable in smaller operations. It had come to be recognized as an axiom that the larger the business the simpler the principles that can be applied to it; that, as the machine is truer than the hand, so the system, which in a great concern does the work of the master's eye in a small business, turns out more accurate results. Thus it came about that, thanks to the corporations themselves, when it was proposed that the nation should assume their functions, the suggestion implied nothing which seemed impracticable even to the timid. To be sure, it was a step beyond any yet taken, a broader generalization, but the very fact that the nation would be the sole corporation in the field would, it was seen, relieve the undertaking of many difficulties with which the partial monopolies had contended."

[THE INDUSTRIAL ARMY] [1]

Dr. Leete ceased speaking, and I remained silent, endeavoring to form some general conception of the changes in the arrangements of society implied in the tremendous revolution which he had described.

Finally I said, "The idea of such an extension of the functions of government is, to say the least, rather overwhelming."

"Extension!" he repeated, "where is the extension?"

"In my day," I replied, "it was considered that the proper functions of government, strictly speaking, were limited to keeping the peace and defending the people against the public enemy, that is, to the military and police powers."

"And, in heaven's name, who are the public enemies?" exclaimed Dr. Leete. "Are they France, England, Germany, or hunger, cold, and nakedness? In your day governments were accustomed, on the slightest international misunderstanding, to seize upon the bodies of citizens and deliver them over by hundreds of thousands to death and mutilation, wasting their treasures the while like water; and all this oftenest for no imaginable profit to the victims. We have no wars now, and our governments no war powers, but in order to protect every citizen against hunger, cold, and nakedness, and provide for all his physical and mental needs, the function is assumed of directing his industry for a term of years. No, Mr. West, I am sure on reflection you will perceive that it was in your age, not in ours, that the extension of the functions of governments was extraordinary. Not even for the best ends would men now allow their governments such powers as were then used for the most maleficent."

"Leaving comparisons aside," I said, "the demagoguery and corruption of our public men would have been considered, in my day, insuperable objections to any assumption

<hr>

1 [From *Looking Backward,* Chapters VI, VII, and XII.]

by government of the charge of the national industries. We should have thought that no arrangement could be worse than to entrust the politicians with control of the wealth-producing machinery of the country. Its material interests were quite too much the football of parties as it was."

"No doubt you were right," rejoined Dr. Leete, "but all that is changed now. We have no parties or politicians, and as for demagoguery and corruption, they are words having only a historical significance."

"Human nature itself must have changed very much," I said.

"Not at all," was Dr. Leete's reply, "but the conditions of human life have changed, and with them the motives of human action. The organization of society with you was such that officials were under a constant temptation to misuse their power for the private profit of themselves or others. Under such circumstances it seems almost strange that you dared entrust them with any of your affairs. Nowadays, on the contrary, society is so constituted that there is absolutely no way in which an official, however ill-disposed, could possibly make any profit for himself or anyone else by a misuse of his power. Let him be as bad an official as you please, he cannot be a corrupt one. There is no motive to be. The social system no longer offers a premium on dishonesty. But these are matters which you can only understand as you come, with time, to know us better."

"But you have not yet told me how you have settled the labor problem. It is the problem of capital which we have been discussing," I said. "After the nation had assumed conduct of the mills, machinery, railroads, farms, mines, and capital in general of the country, the labor question still remained. In assuming the responsibilities of capital, the nation had assumed the difficulties of the capitalist's position."

"The moment the nation assumed the responsibilities of capital those difficulties vanished," replied Dr. Leete. "The national organization of labor under one direction was the complete solution of what was, in your day and under your system, justly regarded as the insoluble labor problem. When the nation became the sole employer, all the citizens, by virtue of their citizenship, became employees, to be distributed according to the needs of industry."

"That is," I suggested, "you have simply applied the principle of universal military service, as it was understood in our day, to the labor question."

"Yes," said Dr. Leete, "that was something which followed as a matter of course as soon as the nation had become the sole capitalist. The people were already accustomed to the idea that the obligation of every citizen not physically disabled, to contribute his military services to the defense of the nation, was equal and absolute. That it was equally the duty of every citizen to contribute his quota of industrial or intellectual services to the maintenance of the nation was equally evident, though it was not until the nation became the employer of labor that citizens were able to render this sort of service with any pretense either of universality or equity. No organization of labor was possible when the employing power was divided among hundreds or thousands of individuals and corporations, between which concert of any kind was neither desired, nor indeed feasible. It constantly happened then that vast numbers who desired to labor could find no opportunity, and, on the other hand, those who desired to evade a part or all of their debt could easily do so."

"Service now, I suppose, is compulsory upon all," I suggested.

"It is rather a matter of course than of compulsion," replied Dr. Leete. "It is regarded as so absolutely natural and reasonable that the idea of its being compulsory has ceased to be thought of. He would be thought to be an incredibly contemptible person who should need compulsion in such a case. Nevertheless, to speak of service being compulsory would be a weak way to state its absolute inevitableness. Our entire social order is so wholly based upon and deduced from it that if it were conceivable that a man could escape it, he would be left with no possible way to provide for his existence. He would have excluded himself from the world, cut himself off from his kind, in a word, committed suicide."

"Is the term of service in this industrial army for life?"

"Oh, no; it both begins later and ends earlier than the average working period in your day. Your workshops were filled with children and old men, but we hold the period of youth sacred to education, and the period of maturity, when the physical forces begin to flag, equally sacred to ease and agreeable relaxation. The period of industrial service is twenty-four years, beginning at the close of the course of education at twenty-one and terminating at forty-five. After forty-five, while discharged from labor, the citizen still remains liable to special calls, in case of emergencies causing a sudden great increase in the demand for labor, till he reaches the age of fifty-five, but such calls are rarely, in fact almost never, made. The fifteenth day of October of every year is what we call Muster Day, because those who have reached the age of twenty-one are then mustered into the industrial service, and at the same time those who, after twenty-four years' service, have reached the age of forty-five, are honorably mustered out. It is the great day of the year with us, whence we reckon all other events; our Olympiad, save that it is annual."

"It is [2] after you have mustered your industrial army into service," I said, "that I should expect the chief difficulty to arise, for there its analogy with a military army must cease. Soldiers have all the same thing, and a very simple thing, to do, namely, to practice the manual of arms, to march and stand guard. But the industrial army must learn and follow two or three hundred diverse trades and avocations. What administrative talent can be equal to determining wisely what trade or business every individual in a great nation shall pursue?"

"The administration has nothing to do with determining that point."

2 [From Chapter VII.]

"Who does determine it, then?" I asked.

"Every man for himself in accordance with his natural aptitude, the utmost pains being taken to enable him to find out what his natural aptitude really is. The principle on which our industrial army is organized is that a man's natural endowments, mental and physical, determine what he can work at most profitably to the nation and most satisfactorily to himself. While the obligation of service in some form is not to be evaded, voluntary selection, subject only to necessary regulation, is depended on to determine the particular sort of service every man is to render. As an individual's satisfaction during his term of service depends on his having an occupation to his taste, parents and teachers watch from early years for indications of special aptitudes in children. A thorough study of the national industrial system, with the history and rudiments of all the great trades, is an essential part of our educational system. While manual training is not allowed to encroach on the general intellectual culture to which our schools are devoted, it is carried far enough to give our youth, in addition to their theoretical knowledge of the national industries, mechanical and agricultural, a certain familiarity with their tools and methods. Our schools are constantly visiting our workshops, and often are taken on long excursions to inspect particular industrial enterprises. In your day a man was not ashamed to be grossly ignorant of all trades except his own, but such ignorance would not be consistent with our idea of placing everyone in a position to select intelligently the occupation for which he has most taste. Usually long before he is mustered into service a young man has found out the pursuit he wants to follow, has acquired a great deal of knowledge about it, and is awaiting impatiently the time when he can enlist in its ranks."

"Surely," I said, "it can hardly be that the number of volunteers for any trade is exactly the number needed in that trade. It must be generally either under or over the demand."

"The supply of volunteers is always expected to fully equal the demand," replied Dr. Leete. "It is the business of the ad-

ministration to see that this is the case. The rate of volunteering for each trade is closely watched. If there be a noticeably
greater excess of volunteers over men needed in any trade,
it is inferred that the trade offers greater attractions than
others. On the other hand, if the number of volunteers for a
trade tends to drop below the demand, it is inferred that it is
thought more arduous. It is the business of the administration
to seek constantly to equalize the attractions of the trades,
so far as the conditions of labor in them are concerned, so
that all trades shall be equally attractive to persons having
natural tastes for them. This is done by making the hours of
labor in different trades differ according to their arduousness.
The lighter trades, prosecuted under the most agreeable circumstances, have in this way the longest hours, while an
arduous trade, such as mining, has very short hours. There is
no theory, no *a priori* rule, by which the respective attractive-
ness of industries is determined. The administration, in taking
burdens off one class of workers and adding them to other
classes, simply follows the fluctuations of opinion among the
workers themselves as indicated by the rate of volunteering.
The principle is that no man's work ought to be, on the whole,
harder for him than any other man's for him, the workers
themselves to be the judges. There are no limits to the application of this rule. If any particular occupation is in itself
so arduous or so oppressive that, in order to induce volunteers,
the day's work in it had to be reduced to ten minutes, it would
be done. If, even then, no man was willing to do it, it would
remain undone. But of course, in point of fact, a moderate
reduction in the hours of labor, or addition of other privileges,
suffices to secure all needed volunteers for any occupation
necessary to men. If, indeed, the unavoidable difficulties and
dangers of such a necessary pursuit were so great that no
inducement of compensating advantages would overcome
men's repugnance to it, the administration would only need
to take it out of the common order of occupations by de-
claring it 'extra-hazardous,' and those who pursued it especially worthy of the national gratitude, to be overrun with

volunteers. Our young men are very greedy of honor, and do not let slip such opportunities. Of course you will see that dependence on the purely voluntary choice of avocations involves the abolition in all of anything like unhygienic conditions or special peril to life and limb. Health and safety are conditions common to all industries. The nation does not maim and slaughter its workmen by thousands, as did the private capitalists and corporations of your day."

"When there are more who want to enter a particular trade than there is room for, how do you decide between the applicants?" I inquired.

"Preference is given to those who have acquired the most knowledge of the trade they wish to follow. No man, however, who through successive years remains persistent in his desire to show what he can do at any particular trade, is in the end denied an opportunity. Meanwhile, if a man cannot at first win entrance into the business he prefers, he has usually one or more alternative preferences, pursuits for which he has some degree of aptitude, although not the highest. Everyone, indeed, is expected to study his aptitudes so as to have not only a first choice as to occupation, but a second or third, so that if, either at the outset of his career or subsequently, owing to the progress of invention or changes in demand, he is unable to follow his first vocation, he can still find reasonably congenial employment. This principle of secondary choices as to occupation is quite important in our system. I should add, in reference to the counter-possibility of some sudden failure of volunteers in a particular trade, or some sudden necessity of an increased force, that the administration, while depending on the voluntary system for filling up the trades as a rule, holds always in reserve the power to call for special volunteers, or draft any force needed from any quarter. Generally, however, all needs of this sort can be met by details from the class of unskilled or common laborers."

"How is this class of common laborers recruited?" I asked. "Surely nobody voluntarily enters that."

"It is the grade to which all new recruits belong for the

first three years of their service. It is not till after this period, during which he is assignable to any work at the discretion of his superiors, that the young man is allowed to elect a special avocation. These three years of stringent discipline none are exempt from, and very glad our young men are to pass from this severe school into the comparative liberty of the trades. If a man were so stupid as to have no choice as to occupation, he would simply remain a common laborer; but such cases, as you may suppose, are not common."

"Having once elected and entered on a trade or occupation," I remarked, "I suppose he has to stick to it the rest of his life."

"Not necessarily," replied Dr. Leete; "while frequent and merely capricious changes of occupation are not encouraged or even permitted, every worker is allowed, of course, under certain regulations and in accordance with the exigencies of the service, to volunteer for another industry which he thinks would suit him better than his first choice. In this case his application is received just as if he were volunteering for the first time, and on the same terms. Not only this, but a worker may likewise, under suitable regulations and not too frequently, obtain a transfer to an establishment of the same industry in another part of the country which for any reason he may prefer. Under your system a discontented man could indeed leave his work at will, but he left his means of support at the same time, and took his chances as to future livelihood. We find that the number of men who wish to abandon an accustomed occupation for a new one, and old friends and associations for strange ones, is small. It is only the poorer sort of workmen who desire to change even as frequently as our regulations permit. Of course transfers or discharges, when health demands them, are always given."

"As an industrial system, I should think this might be extremely efficient," I said, "but I don't see that it makes any provision for the professional classes, the men who serve the nation with brains instead of hands. Of course you can't get along without the brain-workers. How, then, are they selected from those who are to serve as farmers and mechanics? That must require a very delicate sort of sifting process, I should say."

"So it does," replied Dr. Leete; "the most delicate possible test is needed here, and so we leave the question whether a man shall be a brain- or hand-worker entirely to him to settle. At the end of the term of three years as a common laborer, which every man must serve, it is for him to choose, in accordance with his natural tastes, whether he will fit himself for an art or profession, or be a farmer or mechanic. If he feels that he can do better work with his brains than his muscles, he finds every facility provided for testing the reality of his supposed bent, of cultivating it, and, if fit, of pursuing it as his avocation. The schools of technology, of medicine, of art, of music, of histrionics, and of higher liberal learning, are always open to aspirants without condition."

"Are not the schools flooded with young men whose only motive is to avoid work?"

Dr. Leete smiled a little grimly.

"No one is at all likely to enter the professional schools for the purpose of avoiding work, I assure you," he said. "They are intended for those with special aptitude for the branches they teach, and anyone without it would find it easier to do double hours at his trade than try to keep up with the classes. Of course many honestly mistake their vocation, and, finding themselves unequal to the requirements of the schools, drop out and return to the industrial service; no discredit attaches to such persons, for the public policy is to encourage all to develop suspected talents which only actual tests can prove the reality of. The professional and scientific schools of your day depended on the patronage of their pupils for support, and the practice appears to have been common of giving diplomas to unfit persons, who afterwards found their way into the professions. Our schools are national institutions, and to have passed their tests is a proof of special abilities not to be questioned.

"This opportunity for a professional training," the doctor

continued, "remains open to every man till the age of thirty is reached, after which students are not received, as there would remain too brief a period before the age of discharge in which to serve the nation in their professions. In your day, young men had to choose their professions very young, and therefore, in a large proportion of instances, wholly mistook their vocations. It is recognized nowadays that the natural aptitudes of some are later than those of others in developing, and therefore, while the choice of profession may be made as early as twenty-four, it remains open for six years longer."

"I [3] should not fail to mention," resumed the doctor, "that for those too deficient in mental or bodily strength to be fairly graded with the main body of workers, we have a separate grade, unconnected with the others—a sort of invalid corps, the members of which are provided with a light class of tasks fitted to their strength. All our sick in mind and body, all our deaf and dumb, and lame and blind and crippled, and even our insane, belong to this invalid corps, and bear its insignia. The strongest often do nearly a man's work, the feeblest, of course, nothing; but none who can do anything are willing quite to give up. In their lucid intervals, even our insane are eager to do what they can."

"That is a pretty idea of the invalid corps," I said. "Even a barbarian from the nineteenth century can appreciate that. It is a very graceful way of disguising charity, and must be grateful to the feelings of its recipients."

"Charity!" repeated Dr. Leete. "Did you suppose that we consider the incapable class we are talking of objects of charity?"

"Why, naturally," I said, "inasmuch as they are incapable of self-support."

But here the doctor took me up quickly.

"Who is capable of self-support?" he demanded. "There is no such thing in a civilized society as self-support. In a state of society so barbarous as not even to know family co-operation, each individual may possibly support himself, though

3 [From Chapter XII.]

even then for a part of his life only; but from the moment that men begin to live together, and constitute even the rudest sort of society, self-support becomes impossible. As men grow more civilized, and the subdivision of occupations and services is carried out, a complex mutual dependence becomes the universal rule. Every man, however solitary may seem his occupation, is a member of a vast industrial partnership, as large as the nation, as large as humanity. The necessity of mutual dependence should imply the duty and guarantee of mutual support, and that it did not in your day, constituted the essential cruelty and unreason of your system."

"That may all be so," I replied, "but it does not touch the case of those who are unable to contribute anything to the product of industry."

"Surely I told you this morning, at least I thought I did," replied Dr. Leete, "that the right of a man to maintenance at the nation's table depends on the fact that he is a man, and not on the amount of health and strength he may have, so long as he does his best."

"You said so," I answered, "but I supposed the rule applied only to the workers of different ability. Does it also hold of those who can do nothing at all?"

"Are they not also men?"

"I am to understand, then, that the lame, the blind, the sick, and the impotent, are as well off as the most efficient, and have the same income?"

"Certainly," was the reply.

"The idea of charity on such a scale," I answered, "would have made our most enthusiastic philanthropists gasp."

"If you had a sick brother at home," replied Dr. Leete, "unable to work, would you feed him on less dainty food, and lodge and clothe him more poorly than yourself? More likely far, you would give him the preference; nor would you think of calling it charity. Would not the word, in that connection, fill you with indignation?"

"Of course," I replied; "but the cases are not parallel. There is a sense, no doubt, in which all men are brothers; but this general sort of brotherhood is not to be compared, except for rhetorical purposes, to the brotherhood of blood, either as to its sentiment or its obligations."

"There speaks the nineteenth century!" exclaimed Dr. Leete. "Ah, Mr. West, there is no doubt as to the length of time that you slept. If I were to give you, in one sentence, a key to what may seem the mysteries of our civilization as compared with that of your age, I should say that it is the fact that the solidarity of the race and the brotherhood of man, which to you were but fine phrases, are, to our thinking and feeling, ties as real and as vital as physical fraternity.

"But even setting that consideration aside, I do not see why it so surprises you that those who cannot work are conceded the full right to live on the produce of those who can. Even in your day, the duty of military service for the protection of the nation, to which our industrial service corresponds, while obligatory on those able to discharge it, did not operate to deprive of the privileges of citizenship those who were unable. They stayed at home, and were protected by those who fought, and nobody questioned their right to be, or thought less of them. So, now, the requirement of industrial service from those able to render it does not operate to deprive of the privileges of citizenship, which now implies the citizen's maintenance, him who cannot work. The worker is not a citizen because he works, but works because he is a citizen. As you recognized the duty of the strong to fight for the weak, we, now that fighting is gone by, recognize his duty to work for him.

"A solution which leaves an unaccounted-for residuum is no solution at all; and our solution of the problem of human society would have been none at all had it left the lame, the sick, and the blind outside with the beasts, to fare as they might. Better far have left the strong and well unprovided for than these burdened ones, toward whom every heart must yearn, and for whom ease of mind and body should be provided, if for no others. Therefore it is, as I told you this morning, that the title of every man, woman, and child to the means of existence rests on no basis less plain, broad, and simple than the fact that they are fellows of one race—members of one human family. The only coin current is the image of God, and that is good for all we have.

"I think there is no feature of the civilization of your epoch so repugnant to modern ideas as the neglect with which you treated your dependent classes. Even if you had no pity, no feeling of brotherhood, how was it that you did not see that you were robbing the incapable class of their plain right in leaving them unprovided for?"

"I don't quite follow you there," I said. "I admit the claim of this class to our pity, but how could they who produced nothing claim a share of the product as a right?"

"How happened it," was Dr. Leete's reply, "that your workers were able to produce more than so many savages would have done? Was it not wholly on account of the heritage of the past knowledge and achievements of the race, the machinery of society, thousands of years in contriving, found by you ready-made to your hand? How did you come to be possessors of this knowledge and this machinery, which represent nine parts to one contributed by yourself in the value of your product? You inherited it, did you not? And were not these others, these unfortunate and crippled brothers whom you cast out, joint inheritors, co-heirs with you? What did you do with their share? Did you not rob them when you put them off with crusts, who were entitled to sit with the heirs, and did you not add insult to robbery when you called the crusts charity?

"Ah, Mr. West," Dr. Leete continued, as I did not respond, "what I do not understand is, setting aside all considerations either of justice or brotherly feeling toward the crippled and defective, how the workers of your day could have had any heart for their work, knowing that their children, or grandchildren, if unfortunate, would be deprived of the comforts and even necessities of life. It is a mystery how men with children could favor a system under which they were rewarded beyond those less endowed with bodily strength or mental power. For, by the same discrimination by which the father profited, the son, for whom he would give his life, being perchance weaker than others, might be reduced to crusts and beggary. How men dared leave children behind them, I have never been able to understand."

[FROM THE CRADLE TO THE GRAVE] [1]

"How is this distribution [of goods and money] managed?" I asked.

"On the simplest possible plan," replied Dr. Leete. "A credit corresponding to his share of the annual product of the nation is given to every citizen on the public books at the beginning of each year, and a credit card issued him with which he procures at the public storehouses, found in every community, whatever he desires, whenever he desires it. This arrangement, you will see, totally obviates the necessity for business transactions of any sort between individuals and consumers. Perhaps you would like to see what our credit cards are like.

"You observe," he pursued, as I was curiously examining the piece of pasteboard he gave me, "that this card is issued for a certain number of dollars. We have kept the old word, but not the substance. The term, as we use it, answers to no real thing, but merely serves as an algebraical symbol for comparing the value of products with one another. For this purpose they are all priced in dollars and cents, just as in your day. The value of what I procure on this card is checked off by the clerk, who pricks out of these tiers of squares the price of what I order."

"If you wanted to buy something of your neighbor, could you transfer part of your credit to him as consideration?" I inquired.

"In the first place," replied Dr. Leete, "our neighbors have

---

[1] [From *Looking Backward*, Chapter IX.]

nothing to sell us, but in any event our credit would not be transferable, being strictly personal. Before the nation could even think of honoring any such transfer as you speak of, it would be bound to inquire into all the circumstances of the transaction, so as to be able to guarantee its absolute equity. It would have been reason enough, had there been no other, for abolishing money, that its possession was no indication of rightful title to it. In the hands of the man who had stolen it or murdered for it, it was as good as in those which had earned it by industry. People nowadays interchange gifts and favors out of friendship, but buying and selling is considered absolutely inconsistent with the mutual benevolence and disinterestedness which should prevail between citizens and the sense of community of interest which supports our social system. According to our ideas, buying and selling is essentially anti-social in all its tendencies. It is an education in self-seeking at the expense of others, and no society whose citizens are trained in such a school can possibly rise above a very low grade of civilization."

"What if you have to spend more than your card in any one year?" I asked.

"The provision is so ample that we are more likely not to spend it all," replied Dr. Leete. "But if extraordinary expenses should exhaust it, we can obtain a limited advance on the next year's credit, though this practice is not encouraged, and a heavy discount is charged to check it. . . ."

"If you don't spend your allowance, I suppose it accumulates?"

"That is also permitted to a certain extent when a special outlay is anticipated. But unless notice to the contrary is given, it is presumed that the citizen who does not fully expend his credit did not have occasion to do so, and the balance is turned into the general surplus."

"Such a system does not encourage saving habits on the part of citizens," I said.

"It is not intended to," was the reply. "The nation is rich, and does not wish the people to deprive themselves of any good thing. In your day, men were bound to lay up goods and money against coming failure of the means of support, and for their children. This necessity made parsimony a virtue. But now it would have no such laudable object, and, having lost its utility, it has ceased to be regarded as a virtue. No man any more has any care for the morrow, either for himself or his children, for the nation guarantees the nurture, education, and comfortable maintenance of every citizen from the cradle to the grave."

"That is a sweeping guarantee!" I said. "What certainty can there be that the value of a man's labor will recompense the nation for its outlay on him? On the whole, society may be able to support all its members, but some must earn less than enough for their support, and others more; and that brings us back once more to the wages question, on which you have hitherto said nothing. It was at just this point, if you remember, that our talk ended last evening; and I say again, as I did then, that here I should suppose a national industrial system like yours would find its main difficulty. How, I ask once more, can you adjust satisfactorily the comparative wages or remuneration of the multitude of avocations, so unlike and so incommensurable, which are necessary for the service of society? In our day the market rate determined the price of labor of all sorts, as well as of goods. The employer paid as little as he could, and the worker got as much. It was not a pretty system ethically, I admit; but it did, at least, furnish us a rough-and-ready formula for settling a question which must be settled ten thousand times a day if the world was ever going to get forward. There seemed to us no other practicable way of doing it."

"Yes," replied Dr. Leete, "it was the only practicable way under a system which made the interests of every individual antagonistic to those of every other; but it would have been a pity if humanity could never have devised a better plan, for yours was simply the application to the mutual relations of men of the devil's maxim, 'Your necessity is my opportunity.' The reward of any service depended not upon its difficulty, danger, or hardship, for throughout the world it seems that the most perilous, severe, and repulsive labor was done by the worst-paid classes, but solely upon the strait of those who needed the service."

"All that is conceded," I said. "But, with all its defects, the plan of settling prices by the market rate was a practical plan, and I cannot conceive what satisfactory substitute you can have devised for it. The government being the only possible employer, there is of course no labor market or market rate. Wages of all sorts must be arbitrarily fixed by the government. I cannot imagine a more complex and delicate function than that must be, or one, however performed, more certain to breed universal dissatisfaction."

"I beg your pardon," replied Dr. Leete, "but I think you exaggerate the difficulty. Suppose a board of fairly sensible men were charged with settling the wages for all sorts of trades under a system which, like ours, guaranteed employment to all, while permitting the choice of avocations. Don't you see that, however unsatisfactory the first adjustment might be, the mistakes would soon correct themselves? The favored trades would have too many volunteers, and those discriminated against would lack them till the errors were set right. But this is aside from the purpose, for, though this plan would, I fancy, be practicable enough, it is no part of our system."

"How, then, do you regulate wages?" I once more asked.

Dr. Leete did not reply till after several moments of meditative silence. "I know, of course," he finally said, "enough of the old order of things to understand just what you mean by that question, and yet the present order is so utterly different at this point that I am a little at loss how to answer you best. You ask me how we regulate wages: I can only reply that there is no idea in the modern social economy which at all corresponds with what was meant by wages in your day."

"I suppose you mean that you have no money to pay wages in," said I. "But the credit given the worker at the government storehouse answers to his wages with us. How is the amount of the credit given respectively to the workers in different lines determined? By what title does the individual claim his particular share? What is the basis of allotment?"

"His title," replied Dr. Leete, "is his humanity. The basis of his claim is the fact that he is a man."

"The fact that he is a man!" I repeated, incredulously. "Do you possibly mean that all have the same share?"

"Most assuredly."

The readers of this book never having practically known any other arrangement, or perhaps very carefully considered the historical accounts of former epochs in which a very different system prevailed, cannot be expected to appreciate the stupor of amazement into which Dr. Leete's simple statement plunged me.

"You see," he said, smiling, "that it is not merely that we have no money to pay wages in, but, as I said, we have nothing at all answering to your idea of wages."

By this time I had pulled myself together sufficiently to voice some of the criticisms which, man of the nineteenth century as I was, came uppermost in my mind, upon this to me astounding arrangement. "Some men do twice the work of others!" I exclaimed. "Are the clever workmen content with a plan that ranks them with the indifferent?"

"We leave no possible ground for any complaint of injustice," replied Dr. Leete, "by requiring precisely the same measure of service from all."

"How can you do that, I should like to know, when no two men's powers are the same?"

"Nothing could be simpler," was Dr. Leete's reply. "We require of each that he shall make the same effort; that is, we demand of him the best service it is in his power to give."

"And supposing all do the best they can," I answered, "the amount of the product resulting is twice greater from one man than from another."

"Very true," replied Dr. Leete, "but the amount of the resulting product has nothing whatever to do with the question, which is one of desert. Desert is a moral question, and the amount of the product a material quantity. It would be an extraordinary sort of logic which should try to determine a moral question by a material standard. The amount of the effort alone is pertinent to the question of desert. All men who do their best, do the same. A man's endowments, however godlike, merely fix the measure of his duty. The man of great endowments who does not do all he might, though he may do more than a man of small endowments who does his best, is deemed a less deserving worker than the latter, and dies a debtor to his fellows. The Creator sets men's tasks for them by the faculties he gives them; we simply exact their fulfillment."

"No doubt that is very fine philosophy," I said, "nevertheless it seems hard that the man who produces twice as much as another, even if both do their best, should have only the same share."

"Does it, indeed, seem so to you?" responded Dr. Leete. "Now, do you know that seems very curious to me? The way it strikes people nowadays is that a man who can produce twice as much as another with the same effort, instead of being rewarded for doing so, ought to be punished if he does not do so. In the nineteenth century, when a horse pulled a heavier load than a goat, I suppose you rewarded him. Now, we should have whipped him soundly if he had not, on the ground that, being much stronger, he ought to. It is singular how ethical standards change." The doctor said this with such a twinkle in his eye that I was obliged to laugh.

"I suppose," I said, "that the real reason that we rewarded men for their endowments, while we considered those of horses and goats merely as fixing the service to be severally required of them, was that the animals, not being reasoning beings, naturally did the best they could, whereas men could only be induced to do so by rewarding them according to the amount of their product. That brings me to ask why, unless human nature has mightily changed in a hundred years, you are not under the same necessity."

"We are," replied Dr. Leete. "I don't think there has been

any change in human nature in that respect since your day. It is still so constituted that special incentives in the form of prizes, and advantages to be gained, are requisite to call out the best endeavors of the average man in any direction."

"But what inducement," I asked, "can a man have to put forth his best endeavors when, however much or little he accomplishes, his income remains the same? High characters may be moved by devotion to the common welfare under such a system, but does not the average man tend to rest back on his oar, reasoning that it is of no use to make a special effort, since the effort will not increase his income, nor its withholding diminish it?"

"Does it then really seem to you," answered my companion, "that human nature is insensible to any motives save fear of want and love of luxury, that you should expect security and equality of livelihood to leave them without possible incentives to effort? Your contemporaries did not really think so, though they might fancy they did. When it was a question of the grandest class of efforts, the most absolute self-devotion, they depended on quite other incentives. Not higher wages, but honor and the hope of men's gratitude, patriotism and the inspiration of duty, were the motives which they set before their soldiers when it was a question of dying for the nation, and never was there an age of the world when those motives did not call out what is best and noblest in men. And not only this, but when you come to analyze the love of money which was the general impulse to effort in your day, you find that the dread of want and desire of luxury were but two of several motives which the pursuit of money represented; the others, and with many the more influential, being desire of power, of social position, and reputation for ability and success. So you see that though we have abolished poverty and the fear of it, and inordinate luxury with the hope of it, we have not touched the greater part of the motives which underlay the love of money in former times, or any of those which prompted the supremer sorts of effort. The coarser motives, which no longer move us, have been replaced by higher motives wholly unknown to the mere wage earners of your age. Now that industry of whatever sort is no longer self-service, but service of the nation, patriotism, passion for humanity, impel the worker as in your day they did the soldier. . . .

". . . Based as our industrial system is on the principle of requiring the same unit of effort from every man, that is, the best he can do, you will see that the means by which we spur the workers to do their best must be a very essential part of our scheme. With us, diligence in the national service is the sole and certain way to public repute, social distinction, and official power. The value of a man's services to society fixes his rank in it. Compared with the effect of our social arrangements in impelling men to be zealous in business, we deem the object-lessons of biting poverty and wanton luxury on which you depended a device as weak and uncertain as it was barbaric. The lust of honor even in your sordid day notoriously impelled men to more desperate effort than the love of money could."

[WOMEN IN THE NEW SOCIETY] [1]

The personality of Edith Leete had naturally impressed me strongly ever since I had come, in so strange a manner, to be an inmate of her father's house, and it was to be expected that . . . I should be more than ever preoccupied with thoughts of her. From the first I had been struck with the air of serene frankness and ingenuous directness, more like that of a noble and innocent boy than any girl I had ever known, which characterized her. I was curious to know how far this charming quality might be peculiar to herself, and how far possibly a result of alterations in the social position of women

[1] [*Looking Backward*, Chapter XXV.]

which might have taken place since my time. Finding an opportunity that day, when alone with Dr. Leete, I turned the conversation in that direction.

"I suppose," I said, "that women nowadays, having been relieved of the burden of housework, have no employment but the cultivation of their charms and graces."

"So far as we men are concerned," replied Dr. Leete, "we should consider that they amply paid their way, to use one of your forms of expression, if they confined themselves to that occupation, but you may be very sure that they have quite too much spirit to consent to be mere beneficiaries of society, even as a return for ornamenting it. They did, indeed, welcome their riddance from housework, because that was not only exceptionally wearing in itself but also wasteful, in the extreme, of energy, as compared with the co-operative plan; but they accepted relief from that sort of work only that they might contribute in other and more effectual, as well as more agreeable, ways to the commonweal. Our women, as well as our men, are members of the industrial army, and leave it only when maternal duties claim them. The result is that most women, at one time or another of their lives, serve industrially some five or ten or fifteen years, while those who have no children fill out the full term."

"A woman does not, then, necessarily leave the industrial service on marriage?" I queried.

"No more than a man," replied the doctor. "Why on earth should she? Married women have no housekeeping responsibilities now, you know, and a husband is not a baby that he should be cared for."

"It was thought one of the most grievous features of our civilization that we required so much toil from women," I said, "but it seems to me you get more out of them than we did."

Dr. Leete laughed. "Indeed we do, just as we do out of our men. Yet the women of this age are very happy, and those of the nineteenth century, unless contemporary references greatly mislead us, were very miserable. The reason that women nowadays are so much more efficient colaborers with the men, and at the same time are so happy, is that, in regard to their work as well as men's, we follow the principle of providing everyone the kind of occupation he or she is best adapted to. Women being inferior in strength to men, and further disqualified industrially in special ways, the kinds of occupation reserved for them, and the conditions under which they pursue them, have reference to these facts. The heavier sorts of work are everywhere reserved for men, the lighter occupations for women. Under no circumstances is a woman permitted to follow any employment not perfectly adapted, both as to kind and degree of labor, to her sex. Moreover, the hours of women's work are considerably shorter than those of men's, more frequent vacations are granted, and the most careful provision is made for rest when needed. The men of this day so well appreciate that they owe to the beauty and grace of women the chief zest of their lives and their main incentive to effort, that they permit them to work at all only because it is fully understood that a certain regular requirement of labor, of a sort adapted to their powers, is well for body and mind during the period of maximum physical vigor. We believe that the magnificent health which distinguishes our women from those of your day, who seem to have been so generally sickly, is owing largely to the fact that all alike are furnished with healthful and inspiriting occupation."

"I understood you," I said, "that the women workers belong to the army of industry, but how can they be under the same system of ranking and discipline with the men when the conditions of their labor are so different?"

"They are under an entirely different discipline," replied Dr. Leete, "and constitute rather an allied force than an integral part of the army of the men. They have a woman general-in-chief and are under exclusively feminine regime. This general, as also the higher officers, is chosen by the body of women who have passed the time of service, in correspondence with the manner in which the chiefs of the masculine

army and the President of the nation are elected. The general
of the women's army sits in the cabinet of the President and
has a veto on measures respecting women's work, pending
appeals to Congress. I should have said, in speaking of the
judiciary, that we have women on the bench, appointed by
the general of the women, as well as men. Cases in which
both parties are women are determined by women judges,
and where a man and a woman are parties to a case, a judge
of . . . [each] [2] sex must consent to the verdict."

"Womanhood seems to be organized as a sort of *imperium
in imperio* [state within a state] in your system," I said.

"To some extent," Dr. Leete replied, "but the inner *imperium* is one from which you will admit there is not likely
to be much danger to the nation. The lack of some such
recognition of the distinct individuality of the sexes was one
of the innumerable defects of your society. The passional
attraction between men and women has too often prevented a
perception of the profound differences which make the members of each sex in many things strange to the other, and capable of sympathy only with their own. It is in giving full play
to the differences of sex rather than in seeking to obliterate
them, as was apparently the effort of some reformers in your
day, that the enjoyment of each by itself, and the piquancy
which each has for the other, are alike enhanced. In your day
there was no career for women except in an unnatural rivalry
with men. We have given them a world of their own, with
its emulations, ambitions, and careers, and I assure you they
are very happy in it. It seems to us that women were more
than any other class the victims of your civilization. There
is something which, even at this distance of time, penetrates
one with pathos in the spectacle of their ennuied, undeveloped
lives stunted at marriage, their narrow horizon, bounded so
often physically by the four walls of home, and morally by a
petty circle of personal interests. I speak now not of the poorer
classes, who were generally worked to death, but also of the

[2] [Original version has "either."]

well-to-do and rich. From the great sorrows, as well as the petty frets of life, they had no refuge in the breezy outdoor world of human affairs, nor any interests save those of the family. Such an existence would have softened men's brains or driven them mad. All that is changed today. No woman is heard nowadays wishing she were a man, nor parents desiring boy rather than girl children. Our girls are as full of ambition for their careers as our boys. Marriage, when it comes, does not mean incarceration for them, nor does it separate them in any way from the larger interests of society, the bustling life of the world. Only when maternity fills a woman's mind with new interests does she withdraw from the world for a time. Afterwards, and at any time, she may return to her place among her comrades, nor need she ever lose touch with them. Women are a very happy race nowadays, as compared with what they ever were before in the world's history, and their power of giving happiness to men has been of course increased in proportion."

"I should imagine it possible," I said, "that the interest which girls take in their careers as members of the industrial army and candidates for its distinctions, might have an effect to deter them from marriage."

Dr. Leete smiled. "Have no anxiety on that score, Mr. West," he replied. "The Creator took very good care that whatever other modifications the dispositions of men and women might with time take on, their attraction for each other should remain constant. The mere fact that, in an age like yours, when the struggle for existence must have left people little time for other thoughts, and the future was so uncertain that to assume parental responsibilities must have often seemed like a criminal risk, there was even then marrying and giving in marriage, should be conclusive on this point. As for love nowadays, one of our authors says that the vacuum left in the minds of men and women by the absence of care for one's livelihood has been entirely taken up by the tender passion. That, however, I beg you to believe, is something of an exaggeration. For the rest, so far is marriage from being an interference with a woman's career, that the higher positions in the feminine army of industry are entrusted only to women who have been both wives and mothers, as they alone fully represent their sex."

"Are credit cards issued to the women just as to the men?"

"Certainly."

"The credits of the women, I suppose, are for smaller sums, owing to the frequent suspension of their labor on account of family responsibilities."

"Smaller!" exclaimed Dr. Leete, "oh, no! The maintenance of all our people is the same. There are no exceptions to that rule, but if any difference were made on account of the interruptions you speak of, it would be by making the woman's credit larger, not smaller. Can you think of any service constituting a stronger claim on the nation's gratitude than bearing and nursing the nation's children? According to our view, none deserve so well of the world as good parents. There is no task so unselfish, so necessarily without return, though the heart is well rewarded, as the nurture of the children who are to make the world for one another when we are gone."

"It would seem to follow, from what you have said, that wives are in no way dependent on their husbands for maintenance."

"Of course they are not," replied Dr. Leete, "nor children on their parents either, that is, for means of support, though of course they are for the offices of affection. The child's labor, when he grows up, will go to increase the common stock, not his parents', who will be dead, and therefore he is properly nurtured out of the common stock. The account of every person, man, woman, and child, you must understand, is always with the nation directly, and never through any intermediary, except, of course, that parents, to a certain extent, act for children as their guardians. You see that it is by virtue of the relation of individuals to the nation, of their membership in it, that they are entitled to support; and this title is in no way connected with or affected by their relations to other individuals who are fellow members of the nation with them. That any person should be dependent for the means of support upon another would be shocking to the moral sense, as well as indefensible on any rational social theory. What would become of personal liberty and dignity under such an arrangement? I am aware that you called yourselves free in the nineteenth century. The meaning of the word could not then, however, have been at all what it is at present, or you certainly would not have applied it to a society of which nearly every member was in a position of galling personal dependence upon others as to the very means of life: the poor upon the rich, or employed upon employer, women upon men, children upon parents. Instead of distributing the product of the nation directly to its members, which would seem the most natural and obvious method, it would actually appear that you had given your minds to devising a plan of hand-to-hand distribution involving the maximum of personal humiliation to all classes of recipients.

"As regards the dependence of women upon men for support, which then was usual, of course, natural attraction in case of marriages of love may often have made it endurable, though for spirited women I should fancy it must always have remained humiliating. What, then, must it have been in the innumerable cases where women, with or without the form of marriage, had to sell themselves to men to get their living? Even your contemporaries, callous as they were to most of the revolting aspects of their society, seem to have had an idea that this was not quite as it should be; but, it was still only for pity's sake that they deplored the lot of the women. It did not occur to them that it was robbery as well as cruelty when men seized for themselves the whole product of the world and left women to beg and wheedle for their share. Why—but bless me, Mr. West, I am really running on at a remarkable rate, just as if the robbery, the sorrow, and the shame which those poor women endured were not over a century since, or as if you were responsible for what you no doubt deplored as much as I do."

"I must bear my share of responsibility for the world as it

then was," I replied. "All I can say in extenuation is that until the nation was ripe for the present system of organized production and distribution, no radical improvement in the position of woman was possible. The root of her disability, as you say, was her personal dependence upon man for her livelihood, and I can imagine no other mode of social organization than that you have adopted which would have set woman free of man at the same time that it set men free of one another. I suppose, by the way, that so entire a change in the position of women cannot have taken place without affecting in marked ways the social relations of the sexes. That will be a very interesting study for me."

"The change you will observe," said Dr. Leete, "will chiefly be, I think, the entire frankness and unconstraint which now characterizes those relations, as compared with the artificiality which seems to have marked them in your time. The sexes now meet with the ease of perfect equals, suitors to each other for nothing but love. In your time the fact that women were dependent for support on men, made the woman in reality the one chiefly benefited by marriage. This fact, so far as we can judge from contemporary records, appears to have been coarsely enough recognized among the lower classes, while among the more polished it was glossed over by a system of elaborate conventionalities which aimed to carry the precisely opposite meaning, namely, that the man was the party chiefly benefited. To keep up this convention it was essential that he should always seem the suitor. Nothing was therefore considered more shocking to the proprieties than that a woman should betray a fondness for a man before he had indicated a desire to marry her. Why, we actually have in our libraries books, by authors of your day, written for no other purpose than to discuss the question whether, under any conceivable circumstances, a woman might, without discredit to her sex, reveal an unsolicited love. All this seems exquisitely absurd to us, and yet we know that, given your circumstances, the problem might have a serious side. When for a woman to proffer her love to a man was in effect to invite him to assume the burden of her support, it is easy to see that pride and delicacy might well have checked the promptings of the heart. When you go out into our society, Mr. West, you must be prepared to be often cross-questioned on this point by our young people, who are naturally much interested in this aspect of old-fashioned manners."

"And so the girls of the twentieth century tell their love?"

"If they choose," replied Dr. Leete. "There is no more pretense of a concealment of feeling on their part than on the part of their lovers. Coquetry would be as much despised in a girl as in a man. Affected coldness, which in your day rarely deceived a lover, would deceive him wholly now, for no one thinks of practicing it."

"One result which must follow from the independence of women I can see for myself," I said. "There can be no marriages now except those of inclination."

"That is a matter of course," replied Dr. Leete.

"Think of a world in which there are nothing but matches of pure love! Ah me, Dr. Leete, how far you are from being able to understand what an astonishing phenomenon such a world seems to a man of the nineteenth century!"

"I can, however, to some extent, imagine it," replied the doctor. "But the fact you celebrate, that there are nothing but love matches, means even more, perhaps, than you probably at first realize. It means that for the first time in human history the principle of sexual selection, with its tendency to preserve and transmit the better types of the race, and let the inferior types drop out, has unhindered operation. The necessities of poverty, the need of having a home, no longer tempt women to accept as the fathers of their children men whom they neither can love nor respect. Wealth and rank no longer divert attention from personal qualities. Gold no longer 'gilds the straitened forehead of the fool.' The gifts of person, mind, and disposition, beauty, wit, eloquence, kindness, generosity, geniality, courage, are sure of transmission to posterity. Every generation is sifted through a little finer mesh than the last. The attributes that human nature admires are preserved, those that repel it are left behind. There are, of course, a great many women who with love must mingle admiration, and seek to wed greatly, but these not the less obey the same law, for to wed greatly now is not to marry men of fortune or title, but those who have risen above their fellows by the solidity or brilliance of their services to humanity. These form nowadays the only aristocracy with which alliance is distinction.

"You were speaking, a day or two ago, of the physical superiority of our people to your contemporaries. Perhaps more important than any of the causes I mentioned then as tending to race purification, has been the effect of untrammeled sexual selection upon the quality of two or three successive generations. I believe that when you have made a fuller study of our people you will find in them not only a physical, but a mental and moral, improvement. It would be strange if it were not so; for not only is one of the great laws of nature now freely working out the salvation of the race, but a profound moral sentiment has come to its support. Individualism, which in your day was the animating idea of society, not only was fatal to any vital sentiment of brotherhood and common interest among living men, but equally to any realization of the responsibility of the living for the generation to follow. Today, this sense of responsibility, practically unrecognized in all previous ages, has become one of the great ethical ideas of the race, reinforcing, with an intense conviction of duty, the natural impulse to seek in marriage the best and noblest of the other sex. The result is, that not all the encouragements and incentives of every sort which we have provided to develop industry, talent, genius, excellence of whatever kind, are comparable in their effect on our young men with the fact that our women sit aloft as judges of the race and reserve themselves to reward the winners. Of all the whips, and spurs, and baits, and prizes, there is none like the thought of the radiant faces which the laggards will find averted.

"Celibates nowadays are almost invariably men who have

failed to acquit themselves creditably in the work of life. The woman must be a courageous one, with a very evil sort of courage, too, whom pity for one of these unfortunates should lead to defy the opinion of her generation—for otherwise she is free—so far as to accept him for a husband. I should add that more exacting and difficult to resist than any other element in that opinion, she would find the sentiment of her own sex. Our women have risen to the full height of their responsibility as the wardens of the world to come, to whose keeping the keys of the future are confided. Their feeling of duty in this respect amounts to a sense of religious consecration. It is a cult in which they educate their daughters from childhood."

After going to my room that night, I sat up late to read a romance of Berrian, handed me by Dr. Leete, the plot of which turned on a situation suggested by his last words concerning the modern view of parental responsibility. A similar situation would almost certainly have been treated by a nineteenth-century romancist so as to excite the morbid sympathy of the reader with the sentimental selfishness of the lovers, and his resentment toward the unwritten law which they outraged. I need not describe—for who has not read "Ruth Elton"?—how different is the course which Berrian takes, and with what tremendous effect he enforces the principle which he states: "Over the unborn our power is that of God, and our responsibility like His toward us. As we acquit ourselves toward them, so let Him deal with us."

[THE END OF RACIAL AND RELIGIOUS PREJUDICE] [1]

. . . The interweaving lock stitch of a man in conscious mutual interdependence and service with all his fellow members, and its effect to furnish an assimilating power, [can] overcome antagonisms of race and religion which have been so dangerous, and always might be. Some such influence [is] essential in a polyglot nation like ours. Out of it, and the intermarriage of all classes which will follow, will quickly be evolved the American, the heir and offspring, the consummate product of all the races. Some will then no longer be either Jew or Greek, Irishman, German, Swede or Frenchman, but Americans only.

[LIFELONG EDUCATION] [2]

"In speaking of our educational system as it is at present," the doctor went on, "I should guard you against the possible mistake of supposing that the course which ends at twenty-one completes the educational curriculum of the average individual. On the contrary, it is only the required minimum of culture which society insists that all youth shall receive during their minority to make them barely fit for citizenship. We should consider it a very meager education indeed that ended there. As we look at it, the graduation from the schools at the attainment of majority means merely that the graduate has reached an age at which he can be presumed to be com-

[1] [From The Bellamy Collection, Journal 7, Houghton Library, Harvard University.]
[2] [From *Equality*, Chapter XXX.]

petent, and has the right as an adult to carry on his further
education without the guidance or compulsion of the state.
To provide means for this end the nation maintains a vast
system of what you would call elective post-graduate courses
of study in every branch of science, and these are open freely
to everyone to the end of life, to be pursued as long or as
briefly, as constantly or as intermittently, as profoundly or
superficially, as desired.

"The mind is really not fit for . . . [the] most important
branches of knowledge, the taste for them does not awake,
and the intellect is not able to grasp them, until mature life,
when a month of application will give a comprehension of a
subject which years would have been wasted in trying to im-
part to a youth. It is our idea, so far as possible, to postpone
the serious study of such branches to the post-graduate schools.
Young people must get a smattering of things in general, but
really theirs is not the time of life for ardent and effective
study. If you would see enthusiastic students to whom the
pursuit of knowledge is the greatest joy of life, you must seek
them among the middle-aged fathers and mothers in the post-
graduate schools.

"For the proper use of these opportunities for the lifelong
pursuit of knowledge we find the leisure of our lives, which
seems to you so ample, all too small. And yet that leisure,
vast as it is, with half of every day and half of every year and
the whole latter half of life sacred to personal uses—even the
aggregate of these great spaces, growing greater with every
labor-saving invention, which are reserved for the higher
uses of life, would seem to us of little value for intellectual
culture but for a condition commanded by almost none in
your day, but secured to all by our institutions. I mean the
moral atmosphere of serenity resulting from an absolute freedom of mind from disturbing anxieties and carking cares
concerning our material welfare or that of those dear to us.
Our economic system puts us in a position where we can
follow Christ's maxim, so impossible for you, to 'take no
thought for the morrow.' You must not understand, of course,

that all our people are students or philosophers, but you may understand that we are more or less assiduous and systematic students and schoolgoers all our lives."

"Really, doctor," I said, "I do not remember that you have ever told me anything that has suggested a more complete and striking contrast between your age and mine than this about the persistent and growing development of the purely intellectual interests through life. In my day there was, after all, only six or eight years' difference in the duration of the intellectual life of the poor man's son drafted into the factory at fourteen and the more fortunate youth who went to college. If that of the one stopped at fourteen, that of the other ceased about as completely at twenty-one or twenty-two. Instead of being in a position to begin his real education on graduating from college, that event meant the close of it for the average student, and was the highwater mark of his life, so far as concerned the culture and knowledge of the sciences and humanities. In these respects the average college man never afterward knew so much as on his graduation day. For immediately thereafter, unless of the richest class, he must needs plunge into the turmoil and strife of business life, and engage in the struggle for the material means of existence. Whether he failed or succeeded made little difference as to the effect to stunt and wither his intellectual life. He had no time and could command no thought for anything else. If he failed, or barely avoided failure, perpetual anxiety ate out his heart; and if he succeeded, his success usually made him a grosser and more hopelessly self-satisfied materialist than if he had failed. There was no hope for his mind or soul either way. If at the end of life his efforts had won him a little breathing space, it could be of no high use to him, for the spiritual and intellectual parts had become atrophied from disuse, and were no longer capable of responding to opportunity.

"And this apology for an existence," said the doctor, "was the life of those whom you counted most fortunate and most successful—of those who were reckoned to have won the prizes of life. Can you be surprised that we look back to the great Revolution as a sort of second creation of man, inasmuch as it added the conditions of an adequate mind and soul life to the bare physical existence under more or less agreeable conditions, which was about all the life the most of human beings, rich or poor, had up to that time known? The effect of the struggle for existence in arresting, with its engrossments, the intellectual development at the very threshold of adult life would have been disastrous enough had the character of the struggle been morally unobjectionable. It is when we come to consider that the struggle was one which not only prevented mental culture, but was utterly withering to the moral life, that we fully realize the unfortunate condition of the race before the Revolution. Youth is visited with noble aspirations and high dreams of duty and perfection. It sees the world as it should be, not as it is; and it is well for the race if the institutions of society are such as do not offend these moral enthusiasms, but rather tend to conserve and develop them through life. This, I think, we may fully claim the modern social order does. Thanks to an economic system which illustrates the highest ethical idea in all its workings, the youth going forth into the world finds it a practical school for all the moralities. He finds full room and scope in its duties and occupations for every generous enthusiasm, every unselfish aspiration he ever cherished. He cannot possibly have formed a moral idea higher or completer than that which dominates our industrial and commercial order.

"Youth was as noble in your day as now, and dreamed the same great dreams of life's possibilities. But when the young man went forth into the world of practical life it was to find his dreams mocked and his ideals derided at every turn. He found himself compelled, whether he would or not, to take part in a fight for life, in which the first condition of success was to put his ethics on the shelf and cut the acquaintance of his conscience. You had various terms with which to describe the process whereby the young man, reluctantly laying aside his ideals, accepted the conditions of the sordid struggle.

You described it as a 'learning to take the world as it is,' 'getting over romantic notions,' 'becoming practical,' and all that. In fact, it was nothing more nor less than the debauching of a soul. Is that too much to say?"

"It is no more than the truth, and we all knew it," I answered.

"Thank God, that day is over forever! The father need now no longer instruct the son in cynicism lest he should fail in life, nor the mother her daughter in worldly wisdom as a protection from generous instinct. The parents are worthy of their children and fit to associate with them, as it seems to us they were not and could not be in your day. Life is all the way through as spacious and noble as it seems to the ardent child standing on the threshold. The ideals of perfection, the enthusiasms of self-devotion, honor, love, and duty, which thrill the boy and girl, no longer yield with advancing years to baser motives, but continue to animate life to the end. You remember what Wordsworth said:

> Heaven lies about us in our infancy.
> Shades of the prison house begin to close
> Upon the growing boy.

I think if he were a partaker of our life he would not have been moved to extol childhood at the expense of maturity, for life grows ever wider and higher to the last."

IV. THE MEANS OF
SOCIAL SALVATION

[EVOLUTION—NOT REVOLUTION] [1]

We seek the final answer to the social question not in revolution, but in evolution; not in destruction, but in fulfillment.
. . .

Nationalism is not a class movement; it is a citizens' movement. It represents peculiarly neither men nor women, North nor South, black nor white, poor nor rich, educated nor ignorant, employers nor employed, but all equally; holding that all of us alike, whatever our label may be, are victims in body, mind, or soul, in one way or another, of the present barbarous industrial and social arrangements, and that we are all equally interested, if not for our physical, yet for our moral advantage, if not for ourselves, yet for our children, in breaking the meshes which entangle us, and struggling upward to a higher, nobler, happier plane of existence. . . .

The intoxication of a mighty hope should not tempt us to forget that the success of the great reform to which we have set our hands depends not so much upon winning the applause of fellow enthusiasts, welcome as this may be, as upon gaining and keeping the confidence of the law-abiding masses of the American people. To this end we have need to be careful that no party or policy of disorder or riot finds any countenance from us. It is my own belief that on account of its peculiar adaptation to present economic and social states

1 [From *Edward Bellamy Speaks Again!* pp. 48, 176, 177-178.]

129

and tendencies, Nationalism is destined to move rapidly, but it is for this very reason that prudence and conservatism are called for on the part of those identified with it. Our mistakes alone can hinder our cause.

TO A COLLEGIAN [1]

Mr. Smith, who has joined the Nationalists, meets a young collegian who expects to graduate the next week.

Smith: This is graduation week with you, I understand.

Collegian: Yes, the class is launched on Thursday. The last prop is knocked out at noon, and then—ho, for the voyage of life!

Smith: I hope it will be a long and successful one in your case.

Collegian: I don't know about that. The annual newspaper editorials, which are printed along in the commencement season, credit us graduates with an overweening confidence in our abilities to go forth and conquer the world, but, so far as I know our men, that theory is a mistake. The fact is, while we keep a stiff upper lip, most of us feel a little panicky over the prospect.

Smith: I don't doubt it. I know I did, and if I had known what was before me, I confess I should have felt more panicky still.

Collegian: You had a hard time, then?

Smith: Perhaps not harder than most men, but hard enough. I was ten years knocking around from pillar to post before I found anything to do by which I could fairly support myself and think of having a family. I find plenty of

---

[1] [*Talks on Nationalism,* Chapter XXII. The Nationalist Movement, sponsored by Bellamy and his numerous adherents, attempted to establish the social order described in *Looking Backward.*]

men who have had the same experiences. What are you going into?

Collegian: There's the rub. I prefer the law, but I understand that the profession is desperately overcrowded and there is little chance for a fellow who cannot get the business of some big corporation.

Smith: I suspect that is just about true. How about medicine?

Collegian: I've talked with a number of young doctors about practicing medicine, but they all advise me to die some easier death. Really, they say that half the doctors of the country are living on half-rations.

Smith: How about the ministry?

Collegian: No vocation for it. I suppose I shall try to get a little schoolteaching and wait for something to turn up. There were a lot of the men up in my room last night, discussing our futures, and, except a few rich men's sons, we agreed that the outlook for the average college graduate, in the present crowded state of the professions, was drearier than it had ever been before. I've made up my mind that it would have been better if my poor father had not slaved so hard before his death to send me to college. I might have done something in business, perhaps.

Smith: I don't think you need fret about any lost opportunity in that direction. If the professional men are crowding each other uncomfortably, the syndicates and trusts are crowding the businessmen out of existence. Every one of these business consolidations, with which the papers are full, fences up one more field of opportunity to independent business enterprise. A barber's shop will soon be about the only business a man can start without big capital behind him.

Collegian: I used to say that, if worst came to worst, I was strong enough to dig or heave coal for a living, but I see by the papers that there are a million unemployed workingmen in the country, and I'm afraid I should have to take my place at the end of a pretty long cue. In his baccalaureate,

last Sunday, Prex got eloquent about the world's need of
workers and the careers of usefulness that were just begging
us to follow them. What rot! As a matter of fact, the world
doesn't want any more workers, it has got too many already:
too many lawyers, too many doctors, too many parsons, too
many tradesmen, too many mechanics, too many day laborers.
If a man is going to get a chance to work, whether to dig,
teach, or cure people, he has to fight for it. I don't understand it. It is all a muddle. One would think that the world
would welcome workers, for, after all, it is work that makes
wealth.

Smith: Look out, or you'll end by being a Nationalist.

Collegian: What has Nationalism got to say about this?

Smith: It says the last word and the only word in which
there is any help. Under Nationalism the world will welcome
its workers. It will wait for them with eagerness, take careful
account of their powers, and bestir itself, with all possible
solicitude, to find for each the place his tastes and powers
best fit him for, and to extend his field of usefulness as he
shows ability to fill it.

Collegian: Well, that's what we want; but why can't we
have it now without Nationalism? Surely, it is the general
interest that all should find work.

Smith: It is the general interest, but not the individual
interest. Under the present system, the individual worker
depends upon his particular earnings, not upon his share of
the general earnings. His particular interest and the general
interest are in direct contradiction. It is the general interest
that all should be at work. It is the particular interest of every
individual worker that as few as possible should work at his
business, lest the demand for him, and consequently his
earnings, should either be positively diminished or fail to
increase as they otherwise might. This accounts for the
discrepancy between the baccalaureate theory that the world
wants workers, and the difficulties placed in the way of everybody who tries to get work.

Collegian: And what will Nationalism do about it?

Smith: It will identify the economic interest of the individual absolutely with that of the community, by making his income consist of an equal share of what the community makes, instead of consisting, as now, of what he can make out of the community. The result will be that every worker will be as eager to encourage other workers as he now is to discourage them; for every man not employed to the best advantage will be a loss to all.

Collegian: I can see that everybody would be anxious to get everybody else at work under Nationalism, but what motive has he to work himself, since he will be provided for anyhow?

Smith: The obligation to work at some business of mind or muscle would be a law as binding and unavoidable as military service under the German system, and open repudiation of it would, no doubt, be harshly dealt with. But really, I think the pains and penalties of the law would rarely need to be invoked. I imagine the man's comrades could be pretty safely trusted to see that he didn't loaf. I should be very sorry for a worker who, under such a system as Nationalism, should get himself looked upon as a confirmed shirk. His experience, I fancy, would be something like that of an Indian youth who has got the reputation in his tribe of being a coward. A man who loafs, nowadays, is despised, but he hurts nobody in particular, and so is tolerated; but a loafer then would be recognized as a direct burden on every one of his fellows, and a thief of their earnings. No, I think that, what with public opinion in the foreground and the service law in the background, the community under Nationalism would be less troubled with loafers than it ever was before.

Collegian: But what is going to tempt a man to put forth his best efforts?

Smith: The distinction and honors of the state, and the exercise of power.

Collegian: Will that be motive enough without money?

Smith: That is a funny question for a collegian. Is there any community on earth where emulation for distinction is more intense than in a university, and is there anywhere it is more wholly unaffected by money consideration?

Collegian: No; that's a fact.

Smith: It is far more intense, as well as more honorable in the school and university than in business life, because the money measure of effort and of talent is base, unfair, and every way degrading. I fully believe that the sordid nature of the prizes set before men in mature life, under the present system, do more to discourage emulation than to encourage it, and that under Nationalism we shall see honorable ambition become intensified as a motive, beyond any former experience.

TO A PASTOR [1]

Mr. Smith, who has recently joined the
Nationalist Club, meets his pastor.

Pastor: You are just the man I wanted to have a chat with. I understand that you've joined the Nationalist Club, and probably you can tell me something about Nationalism. People are discussing it, and I was thinking of preaching a sermon on it. If I do, I want to get my facts a little nearer right than some of my brethren have.

Smith: I shall be very glad to tell you anything I know, but why don't you join the club and learn all about it? There are three or four ministers with us, so you wouldn't be lonely.

Pastor: Ah, but I'm not quite ready for that. I'm afraid there are some rather fundamental differences in the way we look at this question of perfecting society. If I understand you Nationalists correctly, you expect to make men perfect by improving their environment, while it is the Christian doctrine that if you reform the individual, social reform will follow.

[1] [*Talks on Nationalism,* Chapter XXVIII. See footnote 1, p. 130.]

You say, abolish the wage system; but Christ says, "Ye must be born again."

Smith: Well, why not both? Is there anything inconsistent between Christianity and the bettering of men's environment? Would it be a good answer to an inquirer who was advocating an improved system of sanitation that he ignored the necessity of personal piety? Really, my dear sir, it is totally incomprehensible to me why you should fancy that in insisting on the need of personal reformation you are in opposition to Nationalism. We agree fully to all you or anybody else can say on that theme; but we call attention to the fact that to improve society, not only a good heart but a good plan is necessary.

Pastor: My remark was, I suppose, suggested by having heard Nationalism spoken of as a sort of new religion.

Smith: It is a religion most emphatically, but it is not a new religion. It is the religion Christ taught. It is applied Christianity. It is Christ's doctrine of the duty of loving one's neighbor as one's self, applied to the reorganization of industry.

Pastor: It seems to me there are two sides to that argument. If you are engaged in applying Christianity to society, why, so is the church. Seeing, then, that we are engaged in the same work, why should not you Nationalists turn to and help the church through its agencies, especially seeing that the church is already in the field?

Smith: Because the reorganization of society which is needed to render Christianity possible is an industrial and economic reorganization, which the church as such has hitherto declined to take hold of.

Pastor: But is it so certain that an industrial reorganization is needed for society? May not the church, in dwelling chiefly upon the necessity of personal reformation, be taking the surest though the slowest way to perfect the social condition? You will surely admit that if everyone lived a truly godly life, the industrial problem would disappear.

Smith: Oh, my dear sir, it seems that you could scarcely

make a more vital or complete mistake than this. Go on, by all means, and do all you can to promote personal goodness; but do not delude yourself with the idea that any amount of moral reformation can solve a problem which in basis is essentially economic. If every man on earth were a saint, if all fraud and intentional wrongdoing were banished from business, the moral evils of the business system would indeed be removed, but the fatal economic defects would remain; and, although men would be happier, because better, they would be well-nigh as poor as now. You would think a farmer a fool who would expect to make a living by a bad and wasteful system of husbandry merely because he was a truly good man. But even if it were true that universal moral reform would solve the industrial problem, could you candidly hold out much hope of its being accomplished within any near or calculable time?

Pastor: I am afraid I could not.

Smith: Well, I can. You good men who have a little suspicion of Nationalism as a plan to sidetrack Christianity will recognize, when you shall sufficiently consider the matter, that it aims to clear away obstacles which have hitherto hindered the progress of Christianity and will open to it a career such as the imagination of a saint never pictured. The trouble with the present competitive system of business is that it will not let a man be good, though he wants to. So long as it shall remain, your ministry is destined to be in the main futile. Pardon me; but it is mockery to tell men to live by the ethics of Jesus today. The law you lay down for them the necessities of their wives and children plead with them to disobey, and they do disobey, and let him who is blind blame them. My eyes are at last opened, and I can do so no longer.

Pastor: I feel how true that is. I have that feeling often enough; too often, I sometimes think, for my pastoral efficiency. I will say, Mr. Smith, that you have set some things before me in a new light. I am not quite yet ready to join your club, but I will admit that I am glad that I did not preach that sermon on Nationalism before we had this talk.

If you are right, the Christian church ought to be in this thing.

Smith: The Christian church is bound to be in it just so far as it is Christian, and I do not mean to say that the bulk of its members are not sincere according to their lights. This world-wide movement for social reconstruction on a higher plane, of which Nationalism is a phase, is an infinitely greater thing than the anti-slavery movement; and while the slowness of the church to take the right side on that issue was a blow to its prestige in America from which it has not yet recovered, its failure to take the right side in this far vaster movement would not leave any church worth mentioning. Mind you, I don't say that it would leave no Christianity. The spirit of Christianity is imperishable, and, if the church failed, would find other embodiments. But I do not believe the church will fail. There are a thousand cheering signs that its leaders will not be found sleeping at this new coming of the Son of Man.

[LETTER TO WILLIAM DEAN HOWELLS] [1]

Chicopee Falls, Mass
August 7 1884

Mr W. D. Howells
  Dr Sir

. . . I think that every writer of fiction, when his fancy seduces him too far from this real life which alone he really knows, has such a cause of weakness and uncertainty as Antaeus might have felt when Hercules lifted him into the air, a weakness to be cured with the novelist as with the giant only by a return to earth. If this be true of the novelist, it is yet more true of the romancer, for it is the undertaking of

1 [From The William Dean Howells Collection, Houghton Library, Harvard University.]

the latter to give an air of reality even to the unreal. Though he build into the air, he must see to it that he does not seem to build upon the air, for the more airy the pinnacle the more necessary the solidity of the foundation. . . . It strikes me that the simple necessity of sticking to the life one knows if one would write intelligently, is reason enough why American authors should write as Americans for Americans about America. But this necessity, far from being a limitation, is to my notion the best of all fortunes to those on whom it is incumbent. If I had the genius of Hawthorne, George Eliot or Dickens and could choose the environment from which I was to draw my material, I should by all means prefer of all possible fates to be an American born and bred. I am most heartily yours[.]

Edward Bellamy

[LETTER TO COLONEL THOMAS WENTWORTH HIGGINSON] [1]

Chicopee Falls, Mass
Dec 28 1888

Dear Mr. Higginson

. . . we shall take this subject [Nationalism] up out of the plane of the beer saloons and out of the hands of the blatant blasphemous demagogues and get it before the sober and morally-minded masses of the American people. Not until it is so presented by men whom they trust will they seriously consider it on its merits. The moment they get to the point of seriously considering it, the present chaotic system of industry with its hideous social consequences is doomed.

I am sure you will agree with me that in view of the im-

1 [From The T. W. Higginson Papers, Houghton Library, Harvard University.]

pending industrial revolution, and the necessity that the American people should be properly instructed as to its nature and possible outcome, a profound responsibility is upon the men who have the public ear and confidence. No doubt somehow or other the revolution will get itself carried out but it will make a vast difference as to the ease or peril of the change whether or not it is led and guided by the natural leaders of the community, or left to the demagogues. It was the peculiar felicity of our countrymen in their revolt of 1775 [sic] that their natural leaders, the men of education and position, led it. I hope and confidently trust that the same felicity may attend them in the coming industrial and social revolution and assure an equally prosperous course and issue for the great transformation. As for our politicians they of course will only follow not lead popular opinion. It belongs to the literary class to create . . . and direct that opinion. It is their opportunity, an opportunity such as never came to men of the pen in any age, an opportunity and a duty as well. It appears to me that in spending their time on aesthetic fads [,] love stories, triolets and such embroidery work in ink, they are losing the chance of their lives, like the young man in your *Monarch of Dreams* who didn't wake up in time to go to the front with his equipment. . . .

Yrs sincerely
Edward Bellamy